PRAISE FOR *WALKING EACH OTHER HOME*

"I am going to give everyone I know a copy of *Walking Each Other Home*. This book, this experience, this path of confronting our fear of death, will radically improve their lives, open them to love and presence and joy. Ram Dass and Mirabai Bush show us—beautifully, deeply, and with such humor—how profound and magical our lives can be as we become less and less afraid of death. I love Ram Dass more than I can say, but at least I can manage to say, 'Thank you, thank you, my brother, my teacher, my buddy, for your company as I make my way home.'"

ANNE LAMOTT
author of *Hallelujah Anyway* and *Traveling Mercies*

"A raw diamond of a book. An invitation into love. Of course, it is a how-to manual for dying (and therefore living) and for being with the dying. It is Ram Dass and Mirabai Bush's generous offering to walk us home. But beyond these things, it is an invitation to sit in Ram Dass's presence as he is now. To breathe in the Grace that blows through the Maui air, and that Ram Dass's current state makes space for. If you've ever had the thought that you wish you could sit with Ram Dass, or your own teacher, reading this book is your chance."

HELEN HUNT
actress, director, and screenwriter

"Like beautiful music, you can hear Ram Dass's wisdom and heart full of love and Mirabai's deep harmony."

JOAN BAEZ
musician and activist

"As Time moves through us, wearing out our bodies, it becomes more and more important to turn more deeply within and find the Timeless One in the heart. Ram Dass and Mirabai Bush point out the beauty and love to be found in living with loving awareness of the inevitable dissolution of the physical body."

KRISHNA DAS
singer of *Kirtan Wallah*

"If there's one book that should be on everyone's bucket list, it's *Walking Each Other Home*. Ram Dass and Mirabai Bush share their wisdom on dying, that singular dance we all have on our docket."

DANIEL GOLEMAN
author of *Emotional Intelligence* and *Altered Traits* (with Richard J. Davidson)

"It's a blessing to have such dear friends explore their thoughts and feelings on a subject many of us find difficult. With the wisdom of loving acceptance, Ram Dass and Mirabai Bush share how we might prepare for the transition out of this life. *Walking Each Other Home* transcends any praise that could be given."

SHARON SALZBERG
author of *Real Happiness* and *Real Love*

"Shortly after reading Ram Dass and Mirabai's über-awesome and amazing book *Walking Each Other Home*, I attended a Pacific Film Archive screening of Woodstock. When Joe Cocker belted out, 'I get high with a little help from my friends!' I instantly added, 'I can die with a little help from my friends. Do you need anybody? I just need somebody to love!' Love, love, love *Walking Each Other Home*!"

WAVY GRAVY
activist, entertainer, founder of Camp Winnarainbow

"What a magnificent gift—teachings that soothe our deepest fears—wise, tender, intimate, heart-opening, and full of love. Don't miss it!"

JACK KORNFIELD, PHD
author of *A Path with Heart*

"On long road trips, my mom would sometimes play Ram Dass lectures, and I would pretend not to listen, hoping she couldn't tell how much I liked them. Many years later, after she passed away from metastatic breast cancer, I was lucky enough to spend an afternoon with Ram Dass at his home in Maui. I said to him 'I wish my mom was here. She loved you.' To which he responded 'She is here.' This book made me feel like I was there again, being reminded that love never dies and that our hearts can open even in the depths of grief. If you think at some point you may die, then this book will be an invaluable tool in helping you transform the mind-crushing terror you're pretending not to feel."

DUNCAN TRUSSELL
podcaster, *The Duncan Trussell Family Hour*

"This extraordinary book on being with dying is tender, brilliant, wise, and true. It is a guide and inspiration for a whole and holy living and dying."

ROSHI JOAN HALIFAX
author of *Standing at the Edge* and *Being with Dying*

"This is an astonishing book—a sacred exchange between two old friends, permeated by wisdom and humor, rooted in curiosity and compassion. By holding up the lamp of his own process of letting go of the body with love, Ram Dass is showing us all the way to die. I find myself looking forward to the adventure."

MIRABAI STARR
author of *God of Love* and *Caravan of No Despair*

"In this intimate, brave, and far-ranging conversation between dear old friends, Ram Dass and Mirabai take us by the hand on their journey through living, dying, loving, and ordinary life. With the ease of two old farmers sitting on the porch discussing the changing weather, they range from profundity about dying to practical advice about living, while all along the way, they deliver us lovingly into the present moment. This is one trip you'll want to take!"

JAMES GIMIAN
executive director, Foundation for a Mindful Society

"This is a gorgeous and important offering—practical and mystical all at once. What a relief to ponder living, dying, consciousness, soul, and love as interwoven experiences in and beyond life and time. What a gift to do so with these two wise and beloved teachers."

KRISTA TIPPETT
founder and CEO, The On Being Project;
host, *On Being* and *Becoming Wise*;
curator, The Civil Conversations Project

"Read this beautiful book and feel your fear of death fall away! Dip your toes into the sea of love where Mirabai and Ram Dass are swimming. They invite us to dive in and float peacefully on waves of story, letting their powerful current of wisdom and humor carry us to the loving awareness that is our true home."

TRUDY GOODMAN
founding teacher, InsightLA

"I've never died, but I'm very interested in trying it one day. Thanks to Ram Dass and Mirabai's remarkable book *Walking Each Other Home*, we can all approach the mystery of dying with so much more love, openness, and gratitude than I ever thought possible. If you or someone you love is at risk of dying one day, this book is a must read."

PETE HOLMES
comedian; creator and star of HBO's *Crashing*

"All of life is evanescent—one of the most fundamental living truths, and part of the core human experience of every living being on this planet. And yet, we need wise, compassionate teachers to explain it through their own experiences. And as Ram Dass prepares for his great moment of truth, he continues to teach us with great authenticity and vulnerability. Delightful conversations between two lifelong friends who have explored the path together. A thought-provoking life lesson is packed in these pages for the rest of us."

GOPI KALLAYIL
Chief Evangelist, Brand Marketing at Google;
author of *The Internet to the Inner-Net*

"I became so engrossed by *Walking Each Other Home* that I read it in one day, and I am comforted to know that others understand the journey of moving from ego to soul. This wonderful, intimate, and soul-stirring conversation is a journey of exploring loving, dying, and friendship. The clarity in understanding the transition from ego to soul envelops the reader in loving awareness of the art of living as preparation for dying. This book is an excellent resource for those interested in what it means to live in the place of love."

CAROLYN JACOBS, PHD, MSW
Dean Emerita of the Smith College School for Social Work and
Elizabeth Marting Treuhaft Professor Emerita of Social Work

"Ram Dass and Mirabai have died and been born so many times no one I know seems to be able to remember. They are old and deep, luminous souls—spiritual heroes embracing and serving us all— noble, loving, accomplished, although not without struggles and travails of their own. Yet they haven't always been that way. That's why we can relate to them and their warm, palpable humanity, their Everyman's Dharma and Everywoman's Way, where ongoing spiritual seeking and profound practice comes into play, including loving, serving others, and remembering God."

LAMA SURYA DAS
author of *Awakening the Buddha Within*
and founder of The Dzogchen Center

"Drawing on deep personal experience, as well as the spiritual teachings of Asia, Mirabai Bush and Ram Dass share with us their intimate dialogue concerning death and dying. We learn to differentiate between the impermanent ego and the enduring soul, and how to shift our attention from intellect to loving awareness. In doing so, our fears of loss of body and self are replaced by an awareness of infinite interconnectedness and the reality of soul. This universal theme is approached with great sensitivity and insight, all of which is carried on the wings of a lifelong friendship between these two remarkable human beings. Readers will thank them for their generosity and wisdom."

ARTHUR ZAJONC
physicist and author of
Meditation as Contemplative Inquiry

"*Walking Each Other Home* is an amazing book on the art of living, loving, and dying by two amazing spirits. A much needed teaching for living in this age of accelerated change and anxiety."

"In *Walking Each Other Home*, we are invited into Ram Dass's home; we are welcomed guests listening to an ongoing conversation he is having with his dear friend Mirabai Bush. It is a conversation about coming home to our souls, a journey of loving and fearing and learning and laughing and forgiving and mourning and remembering, of sharing and giving and dying and living on and on. This book, full of wisdom and blessings, is a rare gift you will want to share with the people you love."

"My wife Girija and I followed Ram Dass and Mirabai to India to study with Maharaj-ji. The night before our beloved Baba died, he remarked, 'Tomorrow I will escape from Central Jail.' He may have giggled as he casually predicted his own death. But he was an enlightened being with foreknowledge of his own passing and, apparently, he had a plan. If you are also enlightened or already possess some other kind of get-out-of-jail-free card, you can skip this book. For the rest of us, *Walking Each Other Home* is a gift, a joy, a reset button of the fear and uncertainty that talking about death usually triggers. It is like eavesdropping on an effervescent plot as two more would-be jail-breakers calmly discuss their own escape plans, replete with giggles. I love this wonderful book, its uplifting and profound stories reminding us that we can live each day fully alive while also knowing full well that this stage of our lives will one day end."

"The final words Ram Dass speaks in this book are 'I love you.' Those words sum up his life, and perhaps his purpose, in sharing the truth, compassion, and soul captured in this inspiring, intimate exchange. It is his loving gift to us about the most important thing we will do in this life."

WALKING EACH OTHER
HOME

ALSO BY RAM DASS

Be Here Now

The Only Dance There Is

Grist for the Mill (with Stephen Levine)

Still Here: Embracing Aging, Changing, and Dying

Paths to God: Living the Bhagavad Gita

Be Love Now (with Rameshwar Das)

Polishing the Mirror: How to Live from Your Spiritual Heart (with Rameshwar Das)

ALSO BY MIRABAI BUSH

Contemplation Nation: How Ancient Practices Are Changing the Way We Live (as editor)

Contemplative Practices in Higher Education:
Powerful Methods to Transform Teaching and Learning (with Daniel Barbezat)

ALSO BY RAM DASS AND MIRABAI BUSH

Compassion in Action: Setting Out on the Path of Service

WALKING EACH OTHER
HOME

Conversations
on Loving
and Dying

RAM DASS & MIRABAI BUSH

sounds true
BOULDER, COLORADO

Sounds True
Boulder, CO 80306

© 2018 Love Serve Remember Foundation
and Mirabai Bush

Published 2018

Book design by Beth Skelley and Jennifer Miles
Hand-lettered design by Meredith March
Illustrations © 2018 Sarah J. Coleman

Photo of Neem Karoli Baba by Balaram Das.
Used with permission.

"Love is from . . ." Rumi poem translated by Sharam
Shiva from *Rumi—Thief of Sleep: 108 Quatrains from
Persia*. Used with permission. Visit rumi.net for more
information.

"No coming, no going . . ." lyrics used courtesy of Thich
Nhat Hanh and the Plum Village Community of Engaged
Buddhism, Inc.

Patrul Rinpoche poem from *Enlightened Vagabond: The
Life and Teachings of Patrul Rinpoche* by Mathieu Ricard.
©2017 by Shechen Publications, Inc. Reprinted by
arrangement with The Permissions Company, Inc. on
behalf of Shambhala Publications, Inc., Boulder, CO.
shambhala.com

"Last Leaf" written by Tom Waits. ©2011 by Jalma Music
(ASCAP). Used with permission. All rights reserved.

"For Grief" from *To Bless the Space Between Us: A Book of
Blessings* by John O'Donohue. ©2008 by John O'Donohue.
Used by permission of Doubleday, an imprint of the
Knopf Doubleday Publishing Group, a division of Penguin
Random House LLC. All rights reserved.

"The Day I Die" from *Rumi: The Big Red Book* by
Coleman Barks. ©2010 by Coleman Barks. Reprinted
by permission of HarperCollins Publishers.

Excerpt from "Du siehst, ich will viel . . . /You see, I want
a . . ." from *Rilke's Book of Hours* by Rainer Maria Rilke,
translated by Anita Barrows and Joanna Macy. Translation
copyright ©1996 by Anita Barrows and Joanna Macy.
Used by permission of Riverhead, an imprint of Penguin
Publishing Group, a division of Penguin Random House
LLC. All rights reserved.

Printed in Canada

Library of Congress Cataloging-in-Publication Data

Names: Ram Dass, author. | Bush, Mirabai, 1939- author.
Title: Walking each other home : conversations on loving
    and dying / Ram Dass and Mirabai Bush.
Description: Boulder, CO : Sounds True, Inc., 2018. |
    Includes bibliographical references.
Identifiers: LCCN 2017059912 (print) |
    LCCN 2018027347 (ebook) |
    ISBN 9781683642053 (ebook) |
    ISBN 9781683642008 (hardcover)
Subjects: LCSH: Death—Religious aspects. |
    Love—Religious aspects. | Life—Religious aspects.
Classification: LCC BL504 (ebook) |
    LCC BL504 .R36 2018 (print) | DDC 204/.42—dc23
LC record available at https://lccn.loc.gov/2017059912

10 9 8 7 6 5 4 3 2

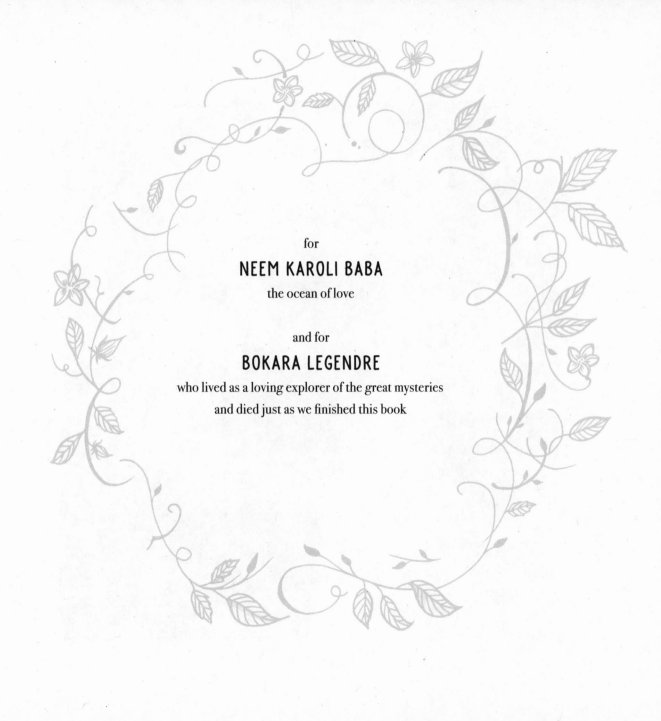

for
NEEM KAROLI BABA
the ocean of love

and for
BOKARA LEGENDRE
who lived as a loving explorer of the great mysteries
and died just as we finished this book

Love is more powerful than death.

NEEM KAROLI BABA

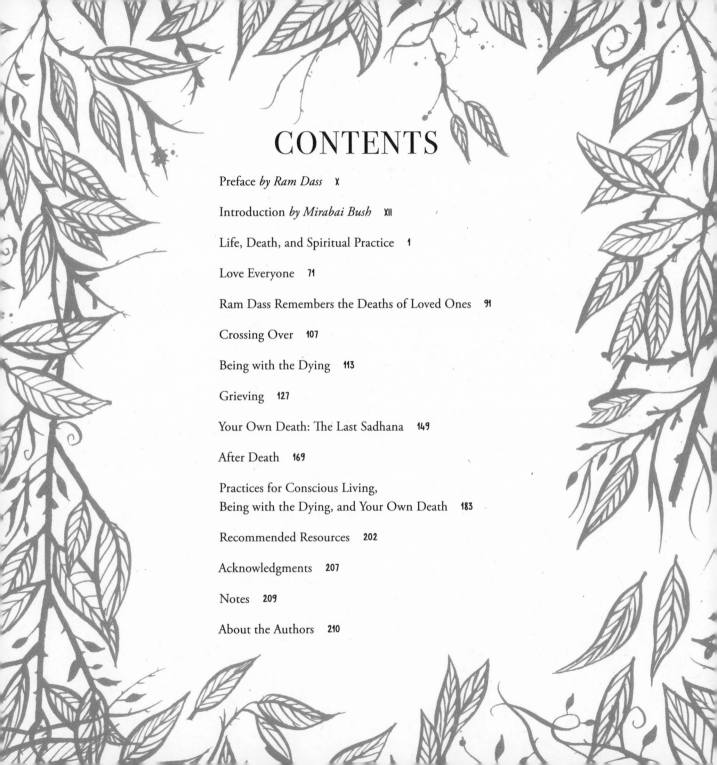

CONTENTS

PREFACE

BY RAM DASS

Dying is the most important thing you do in your life. It's the great frontier for every one of us. And loving is the art of living as a preparation for dying. Allowing ourselves to dissolve into the ocean of love is not just about leaving this body; it is also the route to Oneness and unity with our own inner being, the soul, while we are still here. If you know how to live and to love, you know how to die.

In this book, I talk about what I am learning about death and dying from others and from my getting closer to it, and I talk about what I have learned from being at the bedsides of friends who have died, including how to grieve and how to plan for your own death as a spiritual ceremony. I talk about our fear of death and ways to go beyond that fear so we can be identified with our spiritual selves and live more meaningful lives.

I have had aphasia since my stroke twenty years ago. Aphasia impairs a person's ability to process language but does not affect intelligence. Sometimes I pause for long periods to find a word or figure out how to express a thought in just the right way. I like to say that the stroke gave me the gift of silence. When I thought about the best way to write a book on dying while having aphasia, I knew it would be important to express these ideas and experiences clearly, subtly, truthfully. I realized that these days I have been expressing what I know best when I am in dialogue with another person, someone who is comfortable with silence and listens for new ideas as they arise. Why not create a book that way?

So I invited my friend Mirabai Bush into a series of conversations. Mirabai and I share the bond of being together with our guru, Neem Karoli Baba, and over the years, we have taught and traveled and written together. I thought she'd be able to frame the conversations for you, the reader, and also draw in some of what I've said in the past about dying, while keeping my current words fresh and immediate. And I wanted to discuss her thoughts on dying as well. I also like that this format for the book draws you into the room with us, into this conversation that we all need to have. I hope you learn as much as we did.

INTRODUCTION

BY MIRABAI BUSH

This is a book about loving and dying and friendship. It is a conversation between old friends, in which we talk about love and death in an intimate setting. I hope we've captured Ram Dass's wisdom, expressed in a new way now that he is eighty-six and close to death himself.

As he explains in the preface, Ram Dass had a massive stroke twenty years ago. The aphasia led him to be succinct in his expression—spiritual teaching as haiku. Once, he described the part of his brain that was affected as a dressing room where concepts get clothed in words. Now, when he talks about the mystery of death and what he knows about it, he dresses the concepts simply and gets right to the point.

Ram Dass's journey has been a search for love and for finding a way to stay in the space of love once he experienced it. Our guru, the great Indian saint Neem Karoli Baba (affectionately known as Maharaj-ji), told us to love everyone. This is it, Ram Dass says, the way to live and the way to die. Love everyone, including ourselves. Be in the moment. Be tender, be kind, be generous. Know that we share this journey with each and every person. He has written about love in many books before this, from *Be Here Now*, in 1970, to his latest, *Polishing the Mirror*, in 2015, but not in the way he does here, relating it to dying in surprising ways.

I first met Ram Dass in Bodh Gaya, India, in 1970, at a course taught by S. N. Goenka, the first meditation course taught there for Westerners. Ram Dass was standing at the entrance to the vihara, the House of Stillness, a collection of monk's cells clustered around a main hall. Back then, Bodh Gaya was a tiny, dusty Indian village, home of the Mahabodhi stupa, a stupendous monument erected by Emperor Ashoka some two hundred and fifty years before the time of Christ and situated beside a living offshoot of the actual tree under which the Buddha sat in meditation more than two thousand years ago. Other than the stupa and some small temples, there were few facilities besides the old Burmese vihara. This was where the retreat was held.

We meditated in silence all day, every day. Having been a doctoral student, just looking within was a radical experience for me. Little by little, I got quiet and still. I began to see that I was not only my mind, not only my body. I was those, but I was also awareness. I began to see the impermanence of thoughts and emotions as they rose and fell away, and I started taking them less seriously. I felt much less dependent on the ideas and opinions of others, and it gave me a kind of radical self-confidence, like I belonged here on the planet and would be able to understand how it was all unfolding. That's what it felt like. It gave me faith in the way things actually are and that they are okay even though much needs to be changed. I felt free.

We were American monastics, not what we had expected to be. We had no model for that. In the evenings, Goenka would talk about the Buddha's teachings. Do not dwell in the past. Do not dream of the future. Concentrate your mind on the present moment. Goenka did not talk much about death, except to say that death comes without warning, so make the best use of your time, and that one learns the art of dying by learning the art of living, becoming master of the present moment. We kept watching our breath and sweeping our attention through our bodies.

And then one day, after we'd been sitting in silence with eyes closed for several weeks, Goenka walked into the meditation hall and told us that his teacher, Sayagyi U Ba Khin, had died unexpectedly during surgery in Rangoon. All of a sudden, death, which had come

without warning, was in the room. We were young. We were healthy. We didn't think about death much. But when the course was over and we could speak again, we talked about U Ba Khin and death. We had many ideas about it, but none very clear. I said I thought it would be like falling asleep, maybe the way you drift off into a dream where you are in a wholly different landscape with clouds and doors and a road, but you never wake up. It was Ram Dass who spoke with wisdom. He said that we all are born in each moment and we all die in each moment. With each in breath, we take in life, and with each out breath, we give it up again. We could understand that because we had been paying careful attention to each moment, breath by breath. Then he talked about how Gandhi had died saying the name of God and how letting go of attachment to who we think we are, to what we think we ought to be, to the desire for relationships, fame, material goods . . . how that letting go is preparation for the final letting go of this life. We need to *be* instead of *do*, he said. We need to die as egos so we can live fully as souls, as the Buddha himself did.

Someone said, "But death is saying good-bye to everyone you love so much, to all of this. That is terrifying and catastrophically sad."

Ram Dass said simply, "That's attachment."

Ram Dass had written *Be Here Now* after his first trip to India, where he met Maharaj-ji. While we were learning to meditate, *Be Here Now* was being published in the West. Most of us hadn't seen it yet, but if we had, we'd have recognized its message:

Beyond even conceiving of a place
Beyond which you can go beyond
Who's adventurous enough to want to go
on that journey?
Do you realize when you go on that journey
in order to get to the destination
YOU
can never get to the destination?
In the process
YOU (the ego, who you think you are)
must die
MUST DIE.
Pretty fierce journey. Pretty fierce requirement.
We want volunteers.

One night, under a new moon, I was standing next to Ram Dass on the roof of the vihara, a flat roof where many of us slept on mats. We were talking about our lives and how everything we had experienced was what he later called "grist for the mill." It had all happened to us so that we could wake up, see things as they are. "There are no accidents in this business," he said. "To the ego, it looks like there are miracles and accidents, but there are no real miracles, no accidents. It's just your vantage point that you're sort of stuck in."

I understand that, I thought. *It sounds right.* Then I looked up at the stars against the dark sky—there seemed to be millions of them—and all of a sudden, everything made sense.

The interconnection of everything—I got it, right there in that moment. There is something far greater than we are, and we are an authentic part of it and can contribute to its evolution. I looked at Ram Dass, thinking but not saying, *Oh my god, is this what you meant? This is what it's all about?* He knew what had happened without my putting it into words, and he looked back at me and said, "Yes. And we will all die." And that made sense too.

Ram Dass and I spent two years with Maharaj-ji. Sitting on his wooden bench, just being there, free, Maharaj-ji had nothing, so he had nothing to lose. He loved us unconditionally, fed thousands, and rested in the Presence, never forgetting, always remembering. He loved Hanuman, the Hindu monkey god and embodiment of selfless service. Some thought he *was* Hanuman. To me, he was the tiger of the Kumaon hills—wild, self-possessed, and beautiful. Like a tiger, once he saw you, there was no sense running; it was over before you could even think about it. My heart was lost in his. I had never wanted a guru, but with Maharaj-ji, I realized that it wasn't about attaching myself to someone wiser than myself (although that was a good idea) but about *becoming* myself—and then letting it go. Once a student asked the Tibetan Buddhist teacher Chögyam Trungpa Rinpoche this question: "If it's all inside you, what do you need a guru for?" He answered, "You need a guru to show you that it's all inside you."

After our time with Maharaj-ji, Ram Dass and I returned to the United States, taught retreats, wrote a book together, listened to gospel music in New Orleans, and learned the struggles of our Mayan Indian friends in Guatemala through our work for the Seva Foundation. We both lived with friends in Berkeley and Cambridge and Boulder and Martha's Vineyard and New York. He was godfather to my son and other children in the extended family.

Even in Bodh Gaya, Ram Dass knew the essential truth about dying and living. But since then, after deepening his devotion to Maharaj-ji and having the stroke that left him partially

paralyzed, he has come to see death and dying yet more clearly, through a lens ground by suffering, and his understanding of death is intimately connected to love, unconditional love. Love as a path and a way of being and knowing is called *bhakti yoga* in Hinduism. Maharaj-ji told us to love everyone, serve everyone, and remember . . . remember what is important: remember that we are all one; remember that you will die. And remember God, however you understand that.

Ram Dass moved to Maui in 2004 and has been there ever since, gazing out over the Pacific, teaching retreats, working on books, and seeing students and friends almost every day. Loving everything. His house is a temple, filled with images of Hanuman, the elephant-headed god Ganesh, Krishna, the Buddha, and Jesus and photos of the great saints Ramana Maharshi, Anandamayi Ma, Ramakrishna, and of course Maharaj-ji. There are books and gifts everywhere from friends and students, and three or four purring cats, one of them a black-and-white former stray named Hanuman.

I was visiting one day when Ram Dass seemed a little frailer than the last time we'd met, though his spirit was strong. We were sitting at breakfast, eating papayas and bananas from the garden and drinking tea sweetened with agave, because Ram Dass can't have sugar. Dassi Murphy, who cares for every detail of Ram Dass's life, was there, and Mickey Lemle, the director of *Fierce Grace*, a film about Ram Dass after his stroke. We decide to videotape a conversation between Mickey and Ram Dass to share on Ram Dass's website. When they were ready, I asked: "You two are both such wonderful storytellers, and you have affected so many people with your stories. Why do you think it is important to tell stories to express spiritual truth?"

Ram Dass answered, "Spiritual matters are hard to talk about because they are . . . you can't get the concepts across . . . and, uh"—a long pause—"stories sort of knock on the door of spirit. Stories break through into heart spaces."

Ram Dass has an extraordinary ability to tell his story as an American everyman (or everyperson) as he searches for wisdom and compassion. His story is our story, even if we did not grow up in an affluent Boston Jewish home and teach at Harvard. His brilliance as a teacher and his appeal to a cross-section of people of different ages, classes, races, genders, and nationalities come first from the story of his journey. It is the journey of the ordinary human waking up to discover something is not quite right, leaving home in search of understanding, encountering challenges, facing the inevitability of death, surviving, and returning home to help others by telling his story. And Ram Dass tells it in such an intimate way, by sharing the vulnerabilities and mistakes that precede his learning, that we are pulled right into his narrative as if it were our own.

Being gay in the forties and fifties, he knew what it was to be an outsider, and the outsider in all of us can identify. I wasn't gay, but as a child of divorce in a postwar conventional suburban community, who attended a Catholic school and was called a child of "a broken home," I also felt profoundly outside. Longing for love, desiring to be known for who we really are, wanting to do the right thing and often failing—we all know these things.

Ram Dass has told the stories from his life over and over, and we love to hear them. Sometimes at lectures the audience calls out for their favorites, like they do at a rock concert. "Zumback the tailor!" "Meeting Maharaj-ji!" "Tell us again!" The stories feel good because we know them so well and identify with them. When my granddaughter Dahlia was two, at the end of our reading of *Goodnight Moon*, she would immediately say, "Again, again!" Ram Dass's stories have become like *Goodnight Moon*, like a favorite song, like a mantra—intimate, familiar, reassuring.

But his story is also a send-up of the heroic—a reminder that we are, most of us, living ordinary lives, which makes our individual struggles toward awakening humorous as well as poignant. He uses the stuff of everyday life to reveal the gap between the precept and the reality. He cuts down his own pretensions to show us how hard it is to try to live even the simplest teachings: love everyone, tell the truth, give up attachment to material things. He tells about his jealousy when Maharaj-ji paid attention to others, his desire to drive his sports car after his stroke, his embarrassment at standing in line to see a gay film while being recognized by a student. That could be any of us—jealous, longing, angry, embarrassed. When he thinks he is dying on LSD, his very first thought is not about the meaning of his life but that no one will remember him. This is a universal way of teaching: the story of one person doing his best, failing, failing again, failing better, learning, laughing, becoming, and learning to die.

In 2015, I was visiting Ram Dass in his home in Haiku. We were preparing to teach a retreat called "Open Your Heart in Paradise." One morning after everyone had left the breakfast table, he said, "Let's talk." "Okay," I said. Ram Dass was in his wheelchair. Although he can't walk and can use only one arm and hand, his mind is brilliant. His eyes shone: "I want you to write a book with me."

"Of course," I said, without missing a beat. "What's it about?"

"Dying," he said, "and this time"—and now he was grinning—"we have a real deadline." Then he said, "Sitting by the bed of the dying is sadhana [spiritual practice]. The death of a parent helps us with our sadhana. Dying is the last sadhana. I want to write this together."

Although we both loved Maharaj-ji and have studied with other teachers together, I knew that we each understood those teachings in our own way. Ram Dass is a theist. He believes in God. A Catholic until I was twenty-seven and a spiritual explorer since then, I am more of an agnostic these days: I believe in the possibility of God, but I am more comfortable living with what I have experienced directly—the interconnection of all life, the love that connects us, awe in the presence of this. I wondered if that difference would get in the way of us talking about death.

We had written another book together, *Compassion in Action*, but for that book, we each wrote one section, so it was almost two books inside one cover. That wasn't what Ram Dass wanted this time. "It's about sadhana, spiritual practice, and I want both our voices to be in it," he said. "I want it to be a conversation."

"But I need to ask a basic question," I said.

He nodded.

"Why are we writing this? Who are we writing it for?" I told him that I had recently helped my friend Meng at Google write a book on meditation, and when I asked him why he was doing it, Meng said, "World peace."

Ram Dass laughed. "Did it work?" After a while he added, "I want to help readers get rid of their fear of death. So they can be"—a long pause—"identified with their spiritual selves and be ready to die. If you know how to live, you know how to die. This will be a link between my teachings about Maharaj-ji and about death. And people who are living who can see that they are dying each day, that each day is change and dying is the biggest change—it could help them live more meaningful lives."

As he said that, I remembered that I had just read studies finding that when people become aware of their own mortality, they are more likely to be kind to themselves and helpful to others. And both their close relationships and wider social connections deepen as well.[1]

After a while, Ram Dass continued, "I'm also thinking about people whose loved one has died, who may live with grief, or guilt and regret, and I'm thinking about those beings who are sitting bedside with the dying . . . this could help them prepare for that role. And people who are dying, who could read this book to help prepare them for dying more consciously, more peacefully, being in the moment."

Okay, I thought. *This will be a good book to write. We'll be exploring the edge of what we know.* We liked that the dialogue format would allow his ideas to emerge without the pressure to put them into full sentences and paragraphs. And since our views were different, a series of conversations would be a good form for us to talk about what we knew so far and the questions that remained.

In a review of *Compassion in Action*, one reviewer wrote that we tended "to write in a loving, gushing swoon, as though they are hosting a wonderful party and don't want anything to spoil the mood." It seemed unlikely that we'd fall into a gushing swoon in a book on dying, but we did know that it is a party to which we have all been invited.

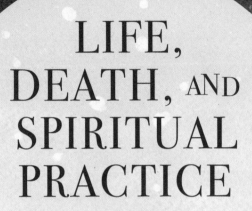

LIFE, DEATH, AND SPIRITUAL PRACTICE

If I'm going to die, the best way to prepare
is to quiet my mind and open my heart.
If I'm going to live, the best way to prepare
is to quiet my mind and open my heart.

RAM DASS

ARRIVAL

On my way to Maui from Western Massachusetts for our first conversations, I am sitting in the cramped space of a Delta flight eating cookies and reading a book by the poet and philosopher John O'Donohue, a friend who had died a few years before. He wrote that paying attention to death reminds us of the incredible miracle of being here, where "we are all wildly, dangerously free."

I think that writing about death will be challenging. Death relates to all of life, so which paths should we take, which stories should we tell, which questions should we pursue? We want to ask questions that will lead to a process of opening and deepening and to an appreciation of how facing death can alter life in helpful and maybe even amazing ways.

Right now I am asking, what do we each *really* know about death, in the midst of this wildly, dangerously free life that we are living? I am not sure, but I know I'll learn a lot from sitting with Ram Dass.

I arrive in Maui late at night. Ram Dass lives in a sprawling house on a hill overlooking the Pacific. His caregivers live there too, and usually old friends are staying as well. Its open floor plan and staircase elevator chair make it easy for Ram Dass to move around in his wheelchair. There are always fresh flowers—hibiscus, ginger, protea, and birds-of-paradise—and napping cats. Everyone is asleep, and I go right to bed. As I doze off, I can hear the quiet whooshing of the ceiling fan and feel the trade winds blowing through the window, ruffling the batiks depicting Hanuman and Ganesh.

To see Ram Dass the next morning after some months away is a return to the home of my heart. As he arrives at the breakfast table, he looks at me from his wheelchair with eyes I have known for so long and through so much. I fall into them and immediately feel happy throughout my body. We hug and then hug more deeply. Beaming. Yes, yes, yes. Over eggs and toast, he asks about my husband, E. J., and his godson, my only son Owen, and my granddaughter, Dahlia, whom he blessed soon after she entered the world. "They are all well. My hip has been bothering me." And I tell him what Dahlia told me: "Ama, you're not old. Old is when you get broken and you can't get fixed."

Ram Dass laughs. As he downs his vitamins and medications, he says, "I guess we're not old. We're still getting fixed."

GOING INWARD

*a*fter breakfast, we go upstairs, where Ram Dass has his bed, a bathroom, his office—a wall of books, photos of friends, an altar with Maharaj-ji's picture, a phone, an intercom. Lakshman, who helps care for Ram Dass, moves him from his wheelchair to a big, comfy reclining chair and covers him with a blanket. The scent of sandalwood from incense burned at the morning chant downstairs floats up into the room.

I jump right in and ask, "You've written and spoken so much about death before this. Do you have a new understanding about death now that you're getting closer?"

Ram Dass closes his eyes and is silent for a long time. I have no idea what he will say. "I snuggle up to Maharaj-ji. I distance myself from the body, my body."

"How do you do that?"

"I identify with the witness, with awareness, with the soul. The body is ending, but the soul will go on and on and on. I keep going inward to the soul."

"Is that different from before?"

"My body is dying now, but I don't feel like I'm dying. I'm fascinated with how my body is . . . doing it."

We both laugh.

Then he says: "For many years, I'd been thinking about the phenomenon of death, but not my own death. I'd talk about it with Stephen Levine and Elisabeth Kübler-Ross, with Frank Ostaseski, Dale Borglum, Bodhi Be, Joan Halifax, and Zalman Schachter-Shalomi, and I'd read the words of great masters and others about death. Now, when I piece it together with my heart, not with my intellect, I find nothing to fear if I identify with loving awareness. Death becomes simply the final stage of my sadhana. My death . . . my death . . ."

Ram Dass is quiet for a long time, looking out at the sea. We've talked about death before, but not so directly and so personally. Saying it out loud changes things.

"For hours I look at the ocean, and I see it as a symbol. It's the ocean of love, and I can just float. It's infinite. I'm getting used to infinite. Time . . . time is just moving, and I am withdrawing out of time. I find myself asking what day, what month, what year this is. But I never ask what moment this is. Ah, this moment. Ah . . . I've been shedding roles, like the role of 'strokee.' I'm doing the work of sadhana: bringing up the past and loving it."

"Loving it?" I ask.

"Loving it as a thought. Letting go of regrets and loving the past for what it was and is. There's a difference between clinging to memories and reexperiencing them from present consciousness. They're all just thoughts. The key is to stay in your heart. Just keep loving."

THE PAINFUL TRUTH

Later that morning, after a break, we begin our next session in Ram Dass's room, exploring what David Whyte calls "the conversational nature of reality." I am tired but so happy to be with Ram Dass that I barely notice. He gets settled in his recliner, with his blanket warming his legs on this overcast and breezy Maui day. Lucian, another of his caretakers, brings us chai that tastes like cinnamon.

The day before, Ram Dass had been sitting with a Brazilian woman who is on a self-retreat in a cabin on the property. She told him about being on a plane that almost crashed and how she had thought she would die but didn't. "It shook her," he says. After the experience she felt more comfortable with death, having been so close to it. Ram Dass says, "That was fierce grace."

Ram Dass has always seen life as a journey of growth and everything that happens to us as an opportunity to learn, awaken, and grow. Learning from a frightening experience is therefore a great gift. He and I begin to talk about how you can get beyond the fear of death if you don't have the good fortune of being in the near crash of a plane.

Ram Dass says, "Well, we are all dying, but nobody admits it. People want a long life. It makes sense; they only know life, not death."

"Remember what Wavy says: 'Death was Patrick Henry's second choice.'"

Ram Dass laughs and shakes his head. Sixties icon and activist Wavy Gravy always makes us laugh, even at the most difficult times.

Then Ram Dass says, "Death is a painful truth. But death is also only a thought. Ramana Maharshi said, 'Don't believe your thoughts. *I am the body* is a thought. *I am the mind* is a thought.

I am the doer is a thought. Worry is only a thought. Fear is only a thought. Death is only a thought.'"

We talk about how we all have fears. Fear begins early in our lives and has helped us survive as a species, originally from being eaten by tigers and now from being hurt in a car crash if we don't buckle up. We fear the unknown: What will happen to us if a terrorist decides to bomb the airport? Specific fears can be helpful—we buckle up. But when we fear death itself—what happens when the heart stops beating—it often becomes a more generalized anxiety, and it can be debilitating. With an anxious and unclear mind, we don't see things as they are, and we can make bad choices.

I tell Ram Dass about my sister's fears as she was dying. "I wondered what fear remained since the dementia had affected her memory so much, so I asked her, 'Are you afraid of dying? Of leaving behind the children you love?'

She said simply, 'I'm afraid.' She showed me her tumor, which was swelling the skin over her liver. She didn't know what it was. Mostly she thought that the swelling made her look pregnant—'at this time in my life!' But she didn't say why she was afraid, didn't mention death. She skipped away from it to make it seem unimportant: 'Well, everybody has fears.' Then she moved to saying there's nothing really to be afraid of: 'If anything happened to me, there are many people here in the nursing home who would come running.'"

But by denying death, my sister didn't change what was happening. She died. We all die, and those people who would come running can't stop death, which Gelek Rimpoche describes as retreating, retreating, retreating, until finally we retreat even from the seed we collected from our parents, into our deepest point.

7

MEMENTO MORI

R am Dass has talked about how our culture supports the fear and denial of death in many ways, from our glorification of youth in the media to embalming practices that make the dead person appear to be still alive. We are discouraged from looking at the bare bones, as it were, of mortality. My mother told us not to talk about "unpleasant things."

Dying most often takes place in hospitals or nursing homes, removed from the natural life of the family. Hardly anyone is simply honest about it, including many doctors, who often consider death a failure in their job of ensuring health and survival even though they know we will all someday be broken and unfixable.

At a retreat for medical professionals in 1989, Ram Dass spoke about this:

> Death is a failure in medicine, and to talk about death as a natural part of life and how to deal with the fear of death and how to stay open so everybody can grow from the process is a departure from the medical model. You've got to move by very gentle degrees. And so my suggestion is you work on yourself. You look at your own fear of dying. And then as you work on yourself and you're lighter about it, your colleagues become interested in what's happening to you. They in turn start to hear it. They may be burning out from being entrapped in failure—because for the medical community, the problem is that all patients die. Sooner or later, everybody dies. I mean, it's just built into the system. And how do you deal with continual failure? Do you keep saying, "Well, medical technology hasn't evolved that far, but later we'll stop that"?

We have to get close to what we FEAR so we know it. Know our attachments, and let them go.

We have to be willing to look at Everything.

The Western religious traditions all tell us to remember that we will die—memento mori. In *The Shambhala Principle*, Buddhist teacher Sakyong Mipham says that "when we feel inadequate, we consume the world around us rapaciously" so that we don't have to think about death.

Ram Dass says, "We have to get close to what we fear, so we know it. Know our attachments and let them go. We have to be willing to look at everything. Keeping death at arm's length keeps us from living life fully." He goes on: "In the Mahabharata, the sage Yudhisthira is asked, 'Of all things in life, what is the most amazing?' He answers that a man, seeing others die all around him, never thinks that he will die. But everyone dies. Each of us will die. We just don't know when."

I say, "Maharaj-ji said to always tell the truth and you'll never be afraid. I guess that means that if you look at the truth of your own death, you won't fear it."

In his classic book *The Fire Next Time*, James Baldwin wonders if "the whole root of our trouble, the human trouble, is that we will sacrifice all the beauty of our lives, will imprison ourselves in totems, taboos, crosses, blood sacrifices, steeples, mosques, races, armies, flags, nations, in order to deny the fact of death."

A WINDOW OF OPPORTUNITY

Ram Dass has written and spoken often about what he has discovered about fear and the denial of death. He has written that as we reduce our fear, we release identification with the ego and connect with the eternal soul. We can give up accumulating experiences and material possessions and instead appreciate the interconnectedness of all things, seeing ourselves as part of a vast oneness, the cosmic fabric.

He has said that the best way to die and to be with the dying is to identify with the soul and not the ego, so we want to start giving up our attachments and live in the place of love. Dying is an incredible opportunity to awaken. It's a window of opportunity. Mechanisms that were serving the ego start to crumble naturally, and as they crumble, there is space. We can expand the space by giving up our attachments, internally and externally, so that we die in a vast space of loving awareness.

Maharaj-ji once said to our guru brother Krishna Das, "The body is perishable! This is not something to be dimly known; it is absolutely true. . . . When a cloth is torn, you cast it away and don't feel bad. When a body dies, it is the same thing. No one can die for another. Everyone must die alone. When someone dies, everyone cries and moans and grieves, but in a few days they are eating and drinking and making merry, as if nothing happened. Why be attached?"

Before we start our conversation again, I decide to listen to a talk on fear Ram Dass gave some time ago. I settle into a big, comfortable chair and put in my earbuds.

Buddha says that fear is the result of ignorance, and the ignorance is that when you start out as an infant with an undifferentiated awareness, you are then taught who you are. That component, which we all call "ego," is a very fragile structure. It seems tough, but it's actually a very fragile structure. It's a structure that is created of mind, of learned neural patterns. This ego is designed to interface between our "impulse life" and society, to protect society from impulse.

When you didn't have a framework, when you didn't have a somebody-ness, you were just part of the universe, and there was no fear. One has to have a self-concept to be afraid, and when an organism is functioning instinctively in a scene, in an infant stage, each change in the homeostasis, each change in the balance of the situation, is just a new moment. It's just a new moment to which it responds.

It's very delicate to interpret things like ego and fear because we tend to interpret from where we're sitting, and we've developed these structures around it. But if you can sense the way it works, just see on one side of you the extremely powerful impulses in you that you may be afraid of and, on the other side, the tremendous forces outside that you may be afraid of, then you can begin feeling yourself as a very fragile entity within the whole structure.

The root of the fear is the feeling of separateness that can exist within oneself. That's where fear starts. Once that feeling of separation exists, then you process everything from either inside or outside in terms of that model. It then keeps reinforcing the feeling of vulnerability because there are incredibly powerful forces moving both inside and outside of you.

The transformative process of spiritual work is reawakening to the innocence by going behind that model of separation that cuts you off, that made you a tiny little fragile somebody. A lot of the power comes from freeing our own fragility.

When you look at social structures, you see how much social institutions are based upon the feeling of fragility within the human condition—based on fear.

You say, "I'm afraid of that person," but you may mean you are afraid of being socially shamed by that person. When you are socially shamed, it hurts, but then, here we still are. Or you're afraid of violence, and then if violence happens, sure, it's scary and painful, but then behind it, here we are.

I think that fear often feeds upon itself, and we're mostly afraid of the fear, which then gives it greater power. But we are just afraid because we think we are vulnerable.

GETTING CLOSE TO FEAR

In the afternoon, we meet again over tea. Ram Dass says, "When I am afraid of something, I come up as close to it as possible, and I notice my resistance. I allow myself to just notice the resistance, because the resistance intensifies the fear—there's no doubt about it. Get as close to the fear as you can, noticing the boundaries of it, just being with it, seeing it as it is. Don't grab, don't push it away, just notice."

I remember that just after my mother had stopped smoking—which she had done for fifty years—she was diagnosed with lung cancer. Soon after that, she started smoking again. She figured she was dying, so she might as well enjoy her life. She hid it from the family, but of course we knew—we could smell the smoke. I tell this to Ram Dass.

"I was so distressed," I say. "How could she do that? So I asked Stephen [Levine] what I should do. He said, 'Buy a carton of Philip Morris and give it to her.'"

Ram Dass laughs. He gets it right away.

I say, "That was impossible for me. I could not do it. It was too horrible."

"But Stephen was right," Ram Dass says.

"Yes. By actually buying the cigarettes, I got closer to my fears and saw what they were. I saw my judgments and desire to control and my denial around her death." I go on to say, "Krishna Das says that going on the Auschwitz retreats with Bernie Glassman helped him bring fear close. He sat there, just bearing witness to his fears of other people and difficult life situations, beginning to let go of judgments, being present with suffering and terrible horror.

"And the Buddha sent his monks to the charnel ground, where there were bodies everywhere in different states of decomposition: freshly dead bodies, decaying bodies, skeletons, and disembodied bones. He wanted them to bring their fear of death close and look at it. Getting close to what you fear takes courage."

Ram Dass says, "Yes. You have to get close to the root of fear, which is ego identification, because as long as you think you are vulnerable, you are going to be afraid. We often think that vulnerability is a kind of weakness, but there's a kind of vulnerability that is actually strength and presence."

"I remember when Owen was born," I say, "a tiny, totally vulnerable baby, and whenever he cried, all the adults who could hear him went to see what was the matter and tried to help. He was actually very powerful in his vulnerability."

THE WANDERING GHOST

What else helps with the fear?" I ask. Ram Dass is quiet. He seems to be drifting off. Then he says, "India. The burning ghats . . ."

Ram Dass has often said that the time he spent in India, especially Varanasi, changed his understanding of death and helped to rid him of his fear. Varanasi, also known as Benares and Kashi, is the spiritual capital of India for Hindus and one of the oldest continuously inhabited cities in the world. In 1897, Mark Twain, who also loved India, said of Varanasi, "Benares is older than history, older than tradition, older even than legend, and looks twice as old as all of them put together."[2] Varanasi is the sacred city of Shiva, the god of transformation. Hindus believe that bathing in the Ganges River there remits sins and that dying there ensures release of a person's soul from the cycle of its transmigrations: you will not be reborn again into this world of impermanence and suffering. Many Hindus go there to die.

Ram Dass says, "The first time I went to India, with David Padua, we stopped in Benares, and I walked the streets and saw people with sickness and disease, lepers, emaciated people with only one cloth wrapped around them squatting or lying in the street. It was shocking. I felt superiority, Western pity. 'Why don't they have hospitals? Why don't they help these people?' I couldn't stand it. It was overwhelming. When I got back to the hotel, I actually hid under the bed. Then I met Maharaj-ji, and I began to understand differently. I returned to Benares alone, and I found that I was no longer the westerner who had been so afraid. I understood that Hindus went to Benares to die, to release their souls. It was a great blessing for them to be there. I walked the streets, and I looked in people's eyes and saw that *they*

pitied *me*! They were secure in being in the right place at the right time, and I was a wandering ghost, not knowing where to go."

"A wandering ghost, Ram Dass? Is that a cross between a wandering Jew and a hungry ghost?"

"Exactly!" He laughs. "I would spend nights on the burning ghats," he continues, referring to the stone-slab steps along the bank of the Ganges, which are the sacred place where Hindus cremate the bodies of the dead in open fires. "The air is filled with prayers, chants, music, and incense. Sometimes there would be bodies burning around me in the dark, lit by the fires. I'd just spend the night there watching them turn to smoke. I could smell the charred flesh. I would watch as the eldest son of the dead person split the skull before the fire consumed the body. I felt like I could see Shiva put his hand out and take the person into his realm.

"India then was a place where death wasn't in the closet. People didn't seem to be frightened of it in the way that westerners usually are. In the villages, people died at home with their extended families. They didn't need a surrogate institution. When they died, they were wrapped in a sheet. The family would call a rickshaw, and they'd put the body on some sticks and wrap it, put it in the rickshaw, and take it to the burning ghats, right through the streets, chanting the name of God: *Ram Nam Satya Hai* [The name of Ram is truth]. Everybody, including children, would stop and notice. Death was right out in the open, a natural part of life. It wasn't an error or a failure. It was part of life."

Ram Dass looks out at the ocean as we sit in silence. A cruise ship glides by in the distance. He says, laughing, "Gambling and drinking and carrying on."

"Almost time for us to carry on at dinner. That's the closest we'll get," I say.

THE BREATH OF LIFE

I go back to my room and sit on my bed. Am I ready to die? Am I afraid? I'm not really sure.

I remember that sometime in the early eighties, I took a drug that made my heart beat like a jackhammer. I tried breathing deeply. It made it worse. I began to panic, my mind raced at the speed of my heart, and I had one thought: *I am going to die. Death is here, and he is knocking on my heart.* After responding for what seemed like forever with, *No, no, no, I don't want to go*, I was still sitting there, my heart pounding, but my mind somehow allowed another thought to arise: *Just bring your attention to your natural breath. It may calm and stabilize you enough to live, and if you die, you'll die more peacefully.* Images of my life began to arise—my husband, Krishna; my friends; my work—and as each presented itself, I said good-bye. *Good-bye Krishna, good-bye friends Sunanda and Anasuya and Maggie, good-bye sisters Jane and Barbara, good-bye Vineyard beaches and our house in Cambridge, good-bye Seva meetings in teepees, good-bye stars and moon.* But when the image of my eight-year-old son arose, I could not say good-bye to Owen, and I began to think, *I have to do whatever it takes to survive this.*

I was not ready to die. I had more mothering to do, more living to do. There is a time when death comes knocking and it is wrong as well as useless to resist, but this, I knew, was not that time. I focused on my breath—in breath, out breath, breathing—nothing else. It began to steady, breath after ragged breath, and I survived.

Anaïs Nin said that we postpone death by living, by suffering, by error, by risking, by giving, by losing.[3] I postponed death by watching my breath. The next day, I was back to being fully engaged with life—but also changed.

HOW FEAR BEGINS

After a dinner of pasta with veggies and fresh bread, we decide to share stories of our first memories of death so we can look at how fear of dying begins. Around the table in the dining room are Dassi, true friend and wise counselor, and Ram Dass's young, strong caretakers, Lucian and Lakshman. They all help Ram Dass lead a full life. In front of each of us is a clothespin with our name on it. We clip them onto our cloth napkins after dinner so we can use them again at breakfast. Big windows look out over the Pacific. It is already dark, and a full moon is rising.

Dassi begins. She tells the story of a seventh-grade boy burning down his cousins' house when she was in third grade in Catholic school in Philadelphia. Dassi remembers the thick smell of gladiolas in church and her fear at seeing the open caskets of three little embalmed children. She remembers another time of being terrified too, when Sister Rita Michael led her students single file to the convent, where she held up each child to look down a laundry chute, telling them that it led straight to purgatory.

We all laugh but know that it wasn't funny then.

The conversation moves like a moth around the room. Lakshman remembers that his aunt died from cancer when he was about five, and no one explained it to him. "Don't talk about it in front of the children." That made it mysterious and frightening. How could someone he loved be here and then suddenly not be here, ever again? There were no answers.

I tell about the death of my friend Walter's father when I was nine or ten. He had gone fishing in a boat with friends. Lightning hit his metal fishing pole and then traveled up the zipper of his jacket, killing him instantly. I've never quite lost the shock of that. Death comes without warning. Learn who you are before it does.

When it is Ram Dass's turn, he can't remember any early deaths. His family didn't talk about it in front of the children either. "I was protected," he says. But he does remember that when his mother died, he was in California. When he returned home, he was in the room with the casket, and his father wouldn't let him see her body. "He said she didn't want others to see her, but it made me feel like an outsider." And he remembers the undertakers arriving when his father died many years later. They put his body into a black plastic body bag. "The way they did it . . . it felt creepy, like they were doing secret things and I shouldn't look. Somehow, that supported my fear of death. Death was hidden. When I saw the way families live in India—grandparents, parents, children, aunts, uncles, all together—it seemed much better. Life and death were a natural part of the extended family."

Lucian says, "There is a movement to replace hearses with minivans so they don't disturb the community when they drive through. Death is hidden."

Postmodern, I think. Minivans somehow don't evoke the sacred. "Please don't take me away in a minivan!" I say, half laughing, half not, as we clear away the dessert plates.

NO SEPARATION

The next morning, we are sitting again at the table. Ram Dass likes to read the *Maui News* while he waits for his breakfast. It reports on the tides and on local festivals, and there are some national news stories. This day, there is a story on the right to die.

As a stage 4 prostate cancer patient, Joe H. has been considering how he might die and knows he could face intractable vomiting and starvation in the final days or weeks of his life. A retired veterinarian, Joe believes he should have the same right that pet owners have to enable their feline and canine companions to die peacefully at home with medication. He was one of dozens of people to testify at a hearing on a bill that would allow adult Hawaii residents with a terminal illness to get a prescription for medication to end their lives. "I've had a good life. I don't want to have a nasty death," he said.

"Everyone is talking about our subject," Ram Dass says with a grin. "Of course, they should have the same rights as cats." He looks across to Kush, his cat, spread out on the couch.

Right next to that story is a report that Donald Trump, campaigning for president, says he will build a wall between the United States and Mexico.

As we identify more with the soul, fear dissipates and trust grows, because the soul is not afraid of death.

I say, "Trump is playing people who feel separate, people who don't feel they have power. He is telling them they are really separate from Mexicans, Muslims, Syrians. There is so much anger in these crowds of people—they are chanting, 'Lock her up!' Thinking of it spiritually, it all seems to come from fear, arising from a sense of separateness, from loss of love and a yearning for security. The stranger as the danger. I was so touched by the Olympics we watched last night. As soon as their race was over, the decathlon athletes began hugging each other, even though they'd been competing minutes before."

Ram Dass says, "They were impressive." After a few minutes, he adds, "The main preparation for dying is giving up any sense of separateness. When you feel separate, it's very painful."

He continues, "Even love, when it is conditional, can create fear. Each time we form an attachment to another human being, it is of course inevitable, sooner or later, that both people are going to die. So in a loving relationship, loss is built in, which makes it precious and frightening at the same moment. We know that everything is changing all the time. And it's uncertain. That can intensify the attachment.

"Many of us have felt the fear of loving too much, the fear and the pain of loving when you know there will be loss. But as we identify more with the soul and remember that we all share the reality of the soul, fear dissipates and trust grows, because the soul is not afraid of death. There is no separation—the soul never dies."

I say, "Remember the time Maharaj-ji sent us away and someone tried climbing back over the wall to be with him? Maharaj-ji said, 'They don't understand; they think I am just this body.'"

"Yes, yes."

THE OCEAN OF LOVE

*L*ater, in Ram Dass's room, we are quietly looking out the window at the ocean. Nothing is permanent. The waves, the light, are in constant transformation. Each wave is new. Watching, we talk again about how we can let go of fear and separateness and simply be present, without judgment, with the reality of death as it is.

I start the conversation by quoting from Zen teacher and friend Norman Fischer. He says emptiness is not the emptiness of despair. It is the emptiness of all limitation and boundary. It is open, released. That "when there's openness, no boundary between myself and others—when it turns out that I literally am others and others are literally me—then love and connection is easy and natural."[4]

Ram Dass says, "Norman is right. Although some moments of union come spontaneously, we can intentionally transform our separateness and invite the experience of interconnection by practicing compassion and love. The more we live in the soul, the more we see love everywhere we look. I have begun to love beings because they just *are*. I am literally *in* love with everyone I look at. When you and I rest together in gentle, spacious loving awareness, we swim together in the ocean of love. It's always right here. There is no separateness, and there is no fear."

DISRUPTING DEATH

Maharaj-ji said nobody dies a moment before their time, and nobody remains a moment after it. Yet no one *wants* to die. People want to live longer because it is what they know. It's in our primitive brain," Ram Dass says.

"The amygdala," I say. "Fight or flight. Survive."

Then I remember something: "Around 200 BCE, the first emperor of China, Qin Shi Huang, accidentally killed himself trying to live forever. He poisoned himself eating mercury pills that were supposed to prevent mortality."

Ram Dass laughs.

I tell him that there is a real fascination with extending life among the engineers of Silicon Valley, where I have designed a meditation course for Google.

"How are they going to do it?"

"Mostly biochemistry," I explain, "studying the genome, reprogramming your DNA, and working on stem cell advances and drugs. Microscopic nanobots that can repair your body from the inside out. They think of it as extending life and also disrupting death. Intel is aiming to have an 'exascale computer' that can operate at the same speed as the human brain. So I guess you could download your brain."

Then I say, "A while ago, I read an article about a scientist at MIT working on supplements to extend your life, and I thought, well, I'll give it a try. I didn't really understand what was in it, but it sounded good. A month's supply for sixty dollars. Of course I didn't notice any change—it's not like ingesting caffeine. So at the end of the month, I thought, I'm not going to renew this."

Ram Dass asks, "You didn't think extending your life was worth two dollars a day?"

"I guess not," I say with a smile.

Ram Dass says, "It's all interesting, but we already know we can extend life by living life fully moment by moment. I don't really desire to extend my life in time because it's all there—past, present, and future—in the moment."

PERFECTLY SAFE

We are quiet for a while, and I check the recorder on my iPhone to make sure it's working. Then I ask Ram Dass, "What do you think specifically has gotten you closer to accepting death and letting go of fear? What has helped you personally?"

"Sitting at the bedside," Ram Dass says right away—meaning sitting at the bedsides of those who are dying, both loved ones and people he didn't know so well at a hospice or a nursing home. "It's one of the ways that is naturally built into life to help us let go of the fear of death, and it's been taken away. But it's there for a reason. I've learned so much that way. My spirit friend Emmanuel said that dying is perfectly safe. It's sadhana for the people who are dying and for the people with them—seeing your fear and letting it go. It's why I started the Living/Dying Project with Stephen Levine and Dale Borglum years ago.

26

Helpers would be doing karma yoga [the path of service], and the dying people would be making their transition from ego to soul, and everyone would be doing their sadhana together, helping each other let go of fear. When I sat, family members would bring me their panic, grief, confusion, and pain, and all I had to do was keep my heart open and not get caught in what was happening. They said they found my presence calming and reassuring."

As I sat there, imagining how calming it must have been for those folks to have Ram Dass near, the death of Mary McClelland came to mind. She was a dear friend to us both, an artist married to David McClelland, with whom Ram Dass worked in the social psychology department at Harvard. Mary contracted stomach cancer and knew she was dying. I remember the high-ceilinged room, Mary in the huge bed, as fragile as a dry leaf and radiantly pale, her long gray hair in a loose braid, David's Agatha Christie mysteries and Mary's Thomas Merton journals stacked on a table next to the bed. As the time drew closer, she would drift in and out of consciousness, often smiling when she returned to us. She seemed to be making visits to another world. On the day after John Lennon died, we sat around her bed, as we did most days. Her eyes were closed for a long time, and then she opened them and looked at us. We asked her what it was like out there. She said, "There's good music there now."

I say to Ram Dass, "When Mary died, there was something in the room that felt so familiar yet so mysterious, a presence, an energy. The only other time I've felt that was when the babies were born—it was the same. There was no tension at all, just energy flowing, a tangible presence of going or coming, like when you know someone is in a room but can't see them. Not scary, perfectly safe, familiar, intimate, present. And something about experiencing that made me know how much it's all part of the same thing."

Ram Dass says, "That's a beautiful example. There's no separation. It's spirit."

I continue, "One of the first things we did after Mary died was go to Cambridge Friends School to get the kids—Owen and Chandra—so they could be with Mary. It seemed so natural.

But usually kids don't see the person who has died. And even if they do, it's more likely to be in the unfamiliar space of a hospital or a nursing home. It's difficult to get over your fear of death if you don't encounter it."

Ram Dass says, "Death has been hidden and medicalized. Doctors often consider death a failure of their job. But death is a natural transition, not a failure."

"Yes. Sitting with Mary's body after she died, I learned that even if a person is frail, weak, hardly there at the end, the difference between that and death is immeasurable. A person may be very sick, almost dead, but the huge difference is not between vibrant good health and fragility—that is a nanodifference compared to the distinction between anyone still alive, however fragile, and that same person dead. Where did she go? Maharaj-ji's question 'Where *could* I go?' began to make more sense."

FINDING EACH OTHER

am Dass is quiet, looking out the window at the sea. After a while, I say, "I just read a book, *Being Mortal* by Atul Gawande, an American doctor, who opens by saying he learned a lot of things in medical school, but mortality wasn't one of them." Ram Dass hasn't heard of Gawande, but he has

thought a lot about death being medicalized, even though he is grateful for the many doctors who helped to relieve his suffering from the stroke.

"My mother's death . . ." he says and trails off, thinking about her.

He has talked about this often. I look through my notes and find a transcript of a public talk. I read aloud what he said about her:

> When my mother—her name was Gertrude Levin Alpert—was dying, in 1966, I sat with her in the hospital quite a bit, and I was very aware that there was a total hysteria about dying. The entire hospital staff and all the visitors seemed to be involved in a huge conspiracy to deny the fact that somebody was dying. As I sat with her, I would see perhaps more than I was supposed to see in the hospital. I would watch the doctors and nurses come in with that sort of professional cheeriness: "You're looking better. Did you have a little soup? Oh, your color's improved! How are your teeth?" They'd tell her, "The doctor's got a new treatment for you," and then they would walk out to the corridor and say, "She won't last two more days." And as it got closer to her death, there were more needles, more tubes, more doing everything to postpone the last breath of life, even though it was very apparent from her aura, her color, and her behavior that she was dying. Here was a woman who had leukemia after her spleen was removed, was down to eighty pounds, and had already taken on the color of death. But they were busy denying it because of the Hippocratic Oath to protect life.
>
> My mother got the incarnation of a Jewish mother. She wanted a family that a good Jewish mother would be proud of. She used her love to try to create that family, expressing her love only when we lived up to her aspirations. My brother Billy was a success in her eyes—a track star and a lawyer. Leonard studied piano

and organ, and he went to Harvard Business School. I had always been a little out of step—psychology wasn't considered as important as law or business—and when I left Harvard, she was very disappointed.

But as I sat with her in the hospital, in a very weak voice she said to me, "Rich, you know, you're the only one I can talk to about dying. Nobody will talk to me about it. What do you think death is about?" Now this was the first time she and I had ever had that conversation. And it happened because we were meeting in such a powerfully private space, the space of dying. And the dying relaxed her need for power and control. I said to her, "Well, Mother, from where I'm looking at you, it looks like a house that's crumbling or on fire. But inside on the second floor, there you are. And I recognize you, and you recognize me, and our relationship hasn't changed even though this body is obviously falling apart. And from what I understand, from my own experiences and my studies, I firmly feel now, deeply and intuitively, that you're not going anywhere. Your body is going to fall apart, but I don't think you're going anywhere." I was saying that partly out of faith, because I wanted it to be that way, and partly out of knowing.

And she went through lines that are characteristic of some dying people: "I've been gypped: I'm only sixty-four, and my mother lived to eighty. . . . I've been unfairly treated by . . ." No, she didn't say God, she said, ". . . by the world." She also said, "I trusted that doctor to do it, and he hasn't done it." She put her faith in the medicine man. The problem is, the medicine man didn't have that power.

And she was a very oral person, very much into cooking and eating and taste. As her sense of smell and her sense of taste left her, which happens as you die, she went through the horrible depressions that can go with losing life. The relatives would bake cookies and extraordinary foods for her, but they all tasted the same to her.

And then her false teeth didn't fit, and the pain was too great, so she'd take them out. But I never saw her without her teeth because she kept a fan in front of her face. She was too embarrassed to show herself without her teeth. That now seems funny to me because Maharaj-ji had only three teeth. He said he didn't need any more: "My gums are as strong as your teeth." He didn't care that people saw him without teeth.

But my mother and I had found each other in that space of trust, of two souls witnessing her journey to death. We were together again, as only two souls can be. The material success didn't matter anymore.

She died in the intensive care ward. They were massaging her heart and doing all that they do in a hospital, but they couldn't keep her alive.

When it came time for the funeral, I felt I should prepare properly, so I took a large dose of LSD. The funeral was in one of the largest temples in Boston. My father was on the board of directors, so there were hundreds of people attending. I kept seeing my mother flying around like a bird; she would land on my shoulder and then fly around again. Everyone looked somber, and the casket was covered with a blanket of roses.

I remembered that on every anniversary my parents, married for forty-four years, would exchange one red rose along with whatever else they gave each other. As the coffin was wheeled by our row, with my father on the end, one red rose fell off the blanket at my father's feet. We all looked at it: my father, who was a very conservative Boston Republican and philanthropist lawyer; my oldest brother, who was also a lawyer; my middle brother, who believed he was Christ; and me, on LSD. As we look at the rose, we all interpret it somewhat differently, but everybody recognizes that it's not nothing. Just as we are about to leave, Dad bends over and picks up the rose.

Then we all get into the big black Cadillac. Nobody says anything because nobody wants to commit himself. My brother who thinks he's Christ finally says, "I guess Mother sent you a final message." And everybody in the car, including my sisters-in-law, agreed. When we got home, my father, who had a very material way of looking at the universe, looked for a way to preserve the rose for all time. It was ultimately encased in a glass globe with liquid in it. In the course of years, since the process didn't work very well, the rose and the water both turned brackish, and nobody in the family knew what to do with it. It moved from closet to closet. Mother was gone, but the rose survived. I found it much later in the back of Dad's garage, and I put it on my altar as a reminder of the impermanent nature of physical life.

We stop and think about that. "I love the rose," I say. "I thought of Muhammad Ali's death. 'Float like a butterfly, sting like a bee.' When he died, his family flew with his body from Scottsdale to return him to Louisville. Taking him home felt good, right. And then they found out that while they were on the plane, twenty thousand bees had filled a tree outside of the Ali Center in Louisville. His sister felt like he was connecting with them."

Ram Dass smiles. "That talk I had with my mother in the hospital—I felt free because I was on drugs. It was serendipity. I had come from the Newport Jazz Festival, where Maynard Ferguson was playing. I was on mescaline, and she was on hospital drugs. We didn't really talk much about the idea of dying; we talked about the situation in the moment."

"And that helped her, didn't it?"

"Yes. And we noted how much anxiety about death the visitors had. She and I were in a bubble of consciousness. We were the witness. The doctors who were coming and going—they were trying to keep her alive—and death was unspoken in the whole scene."

BEING HERE NOW

We sit in silence for a long while, looking out at the ocean, the sky, and then a small plane flying through the clouds.

Ram Dass says, "When planes go by now, I am piloting the plane. You have to be so busy as a pilot—the radio, the dials, the controls, keeping it upright, and you are looking out for traffic. When you are in the plane, clouds are a negative thing. I am so glad to be here, and not there. I can just look at the clouds and love them." Ram Dass laughs a contented laugh.

"You did used to love flying, when you were a pilot . . ."

"I loved it. I absolutely loved it, but I'm glad I am right here now."

"Me too."

BARE BONES

I go back to my room to check my email, but I can't concentrate. I lie down on the bed and stare at the ceiling. How much am I really afraid? I'm not sure. I think I'm not very afraid to die, but I want to see Dahlia grow up. But maybe I am deluding myself. I feel restless.

Since my sister died, I've been telling myself that she died younger than I am now because she led a really different life from me, drinking more and smoking, not taking care of herself. I've been so much better, I think, doing yoga and meditation for forty years, eating organic food, using the treadmill and hand weights, taking calcium and vitamin D, living healthfully and preparing for death. Her condition belonged to her, not to me, who conscientiously reads about ultralongevity and dharma teachings. But the truth is, I am only six years younger than Barbara, and who knows how and when I will die. Maybe she and my mother both had cancer, not just because they smoked—maybe I'll get it too. Maybe I'm the one who is in denial. Maybe, as Kalu Rinpoche said, I should meditate more. Death comes without warning.

I remember something I read this morning by Pema Chödrön:

"Come back to square one, just the minimum bare bones. Relaxing with the present moment, relaxing with hopelessness, relaxing with death, not resisting the fact that things end, that things pass, that things have no lasting substance, that everything is changing all the time—that is the basic message."[5]

Ram Dass often quotes Carlos Castaneda's books, where Don Juan says to keep death over your left shoulder—just staying with each moment as it is, realizing that life and death are right here all the time. Death is the only wise advisor that we have, according to Don Juan. Remember that life is precious. Preciousness doesn't mean that it is supposed to go on forever. It means that when you are in the present for even a moment, it's precious. There's no time and space in the moment, but there is immortality. "You have to be silent and listen to the quiet callings of the heart. And know that anything can happen."[6]

We resist change. We fear the unknown. But everything is changing all the time—the waves, the clouds, and us. If we are quiet and still in the moment, we can witness change and accept it as inevitable. We can learn to surrender into it, become friends with it. That doesn't mean that we don't work to relieve suffering within that change—we might, for example, do everything we can to heal ourselves or others from cancer, but we try not to deny or become angry that the cancer is there. We can acknowledge it, look at the choices we have, and then act in a loving way.

SUFFERING IS GRACE

Later that day, after lunch, we meet again. I'm a little tired from worrying about whether I am in denial, but Ram Dass has extraordinary energy for someone who had a cerebral hemorrhage twenty years ago (so massive his doctors thought he had only a 10 percent chance of survival; three hospitals and hundreds of hours of rehab later, he was able to go home in his wheelchair).

We settle in. Arrange his blanket. Get comfortable. Outside, the palm fronds are reflecting the afternoon sun. We have a long way to go, but it doesn't feel rushed. We are being here now.

I tell Ram Dass that since we started working on this book, I have been experiencing less fear of death. "I mean, I didn't think I had much fear before, but of course there was some. But I've been noticing that the more I sit with death and read about it and do the practices, the more accepting I feel. Sometimes as I am going to sleep, I imagine I am dying, gently letting go. Somehow allowing myself to be closer to it has changed things."

"So what else has taken you closer to letting go of fear?" I ask him. I am trying to ask questions with a genuine openness, not assuming I already know the answer.

Ram Dass is quiet for a long time. I can feel that he is trying to answer what he thinks in this moment, not the many answers he has given in the past. "The stroke really took me close to death. I saw that, and I survived. That suffering cleaned out some pockets of fear. The suffering didn't make me more fearful, it made me more real. Since then, I'm closer to Maharaj-ji. Soul to soul. I know now that as souls we are unchangeable, beautiful, completely aware, and continue no matter what."

I think, *What more could I ask?*

Ram Dass continues, "When Maharaj-ji was still alive, K. K. Shah and I went to his temple in Kainchi one evening and had this very quiet sitting with him. Maharaj-ji said to K. K., 'I will do something for him,' meaning me. I wondered for a long time what that could be. After the stroke, when I was bottoming out, K. K. reminded me of Maharaj-ji's promise to do something for me, and I thought that the something must be the stroke. I thought that was Maharaj-ji's gift, his blessing.

"I thought it was, but then Siddhi Ma [Maharaj-ji left his *satsang* in her care] watched the movie *Fierce Grace*, in which I said that the stroke was his blessing, and she said, 'Ram Dass ought to be ashamed! Maharaj-ji would never give him a stroke. The stroke was natural, and the grace to live with the stroke and learn from it was Maharaj-ji's gift.' So that's what I understand now.

"Once, I was with Maharaj-ji when a devotee walked up and said, crying, 'My whole life is suffering.' Maharaj-ji said, 'I love suffering. It brings me closer to God.' Then we stood there, quietly, and I wondered how suffering brings you closer to God. But somehow just the thought of that—without any direct answer—helped me.

"The stroke—the suffering and the rage—was for spiritual healing, for cutting through fear, for getting closer to God. I had to learn to accept it. Healing is not about getting back

Suffering didn't make me more fearful; IT MADE ME MORE REAL.

to the way things were, but about learning to live with how they are. Now, although my outer life is radically altered, I don't see myself as a stroke victim. I see myself as a soul. I am not my ego; I am a soul. Or as C. S. Lewis said, 'I don't have a soul; I *am* a soul. I *have* a body.' And having gone through the stroke, the other parts of aging don't seem bad at all. I am not afraid. Suffering is grace."

For Ram Dass, life is a process of discovery, a dance of impermanence, the only dance there is. When we were apart over the many years of our friendship, especially if either of us had been investigating some new practice or teacher or sacred place, we would compare notes about what we had learned, how it had changed what we thought to be true. What was sitting in Burma with U Pandita like? Did he really ask you which part of the breath you fell asleep on, the in breath or the out breath? How was it to fast for three weeks in the Alps? What about childbirth?

Then in 1997, while writing what he believed would be the last chapter of *Still Here*, Ram Dass experienced what many of us have thought we'd experience when writing a book: a stroke. And it changed his life.

When I visited him a few weeks later at the Kaiser Foundation Rehabilitation Center in Vallejo, California, he was lying in a hospital bed, pale, paralyzed on one side, looking at a picture of Maharaj-ji and a batik wall hanging of Hanuman, the son of Vayu, the Hindu wind god, the spirit of breath. After a long silence together, he looked at me, moving his hand as if he were about to speak, pointing to his paralyzed side and then trying to express something that he wanted me to hear. It felt very familiar, even in that sterile room, through my tears. Then he moved his fingers down his arm, like in the old Yellow Pages ads: his fingers were doing the walking. It was the path, the journey.

"Learning," he said. Long silence. "Learning . . . patience. Patience." Then he closed his eyes.

Buddhists say that patience is the antidote to anger. Ram Dass would call on it often as he recovered from his stroke.

THE SOUL NEVER DIES

Back in his room in Maui, now able to speak pretty freely for someone with aphasia and with great patience when he struggles to find a word, Ram Dass says, "Let's talk about fear some more."

"Okay."

"When you identify as a soul, you don't fear death, because the soul doesn't die. I identify as a soul now. I'm not afraid," he says.

"But most of us are," I say. "I called home this morning and asked E. J., out of the blue, 'What are you afraid of?' He said, 'I don't know.' 'Well, think about it.' 'I don't want to think about it—it will make me afraid.' And then, with a touch of irony, he said, 'That's the problem, isn't it?'"

Ram Dass and I both laugh.

Then Ram Dass says, "Death is under the covers. We should replace those covers with Maharaj-ji's blanket. No fear." Maharaj-ji was famous for having nothing but a brass water jug and his plaid wool blanket.

At other times, Ram Dass had also given talks about fear and the soul. Once he said:

We fear the loss of our identity, our individuality, our self as knower. Give it all up, and you come to know the soul. Knowing the soul isn't about knowing anything esoteric or unknowable; it's about releasing your need to know in the conventional way, giving up your sense of separation.

The soul teaches us that the root of fear is separateness. If we want to be free, we have to overcome separateness. But usually it feels like you are yelling out of your room, and I am yelling out of mine. Even trying to get out of the room invests the room with reality. Who am I? The room that the mind built. Yet we've all had times when there was no room, no fear. The moment of crisis, when we forget ourselves and do just what is needed. For surfers, it is the moment when they come into equilibrium with the incredible force of the water. For skiers, it is when the balance is perfect. But we explain it away, ignore it, or let it pass. We each come out of that room in our own ways, again and again. We turn and look and realize we're out—and we panic. We run back in the room, close the door, panting heavily. *Now I know where I am,* we think. *I'm back home. Alone. Safe.* No matter how squalid the room.

REWRITING LIFE INSTRUCTIONS

I am thinking of next questions to ask Ram Dass when that suddenly becomes unnecessary. He says, "LSD."

Of course!

"I glimpsed death a few times through psychedelics. Those times rewrote my life instructions."

I want to hear Ram Dass tell about his experiences, even though I've heard them before. He is, after all, one of the greatest living explorers of the psychedelic universe. And although psychedelics were considered too dangerous for many years by the government, researchers at Johns Hopkins University, New York University, and the University of California, San Francisco, are now finally exploring ways to help people let go of fear and face death by using psychedelics in controlled environments. They are also being used to help people recover from addictions and live better with posttraumatic stress.

One participant in a psilocybin session at Johns Hopkins said, "It sort of eliminates the fear of death as you realize that all things—meaning everything everywhere since the beginning of time—are connected and one."[7]

An assistant guide from the Johns Hopkins program said, "This ego, with all our memories and associations, is what we cling to in the face of death. In the psilocybin experience, there is a loosening of all those connections. The person who goes through the psilocybin journey is less attached and less afraid of death."[8]

"Tell me about the times on psychedelics," I say.

"My first experience was with Sandoz psilocybin, at Tim [Leary]'s house in Newton. A few hours after taking it, I left Tim and Allen [Ginsberg] in the kitchen and went into the living room. In the darkness, I saw a figure standing about eight feet away from me, where a moment before there had been no one. I looked at it, and it was me, in a cap and gown and hood, a professor. It was as if the professor part of me had separated itself from me. *Well*, I thought, *I worked hard to get that status, but I don't really need it.* Then the figure changed: it became that part of me that was social and sophisticated. *Okay, so that goes too*, I thought. The figure kept changing, and I saw all the different aspects I thought were me: pilot, cellist, lover . . . I kept reassuring myself that I didn't need each part.

"Then the figure became Richard Alpert, my basic identity. I wasn't sure I could do without that. *What should I do? Should I call Tim?* But then I thought, *What the hell? I'll give up being Richard Alpert. I'll get a new identity. At least I have my body.* Then I looked down and watched the progressive disappearance of my body. *Oh no! I must be dying. I need my body!* Panic mounted. But then an intimate voice asked very quietly, 'But who's minding the store?' I realized that although everything I knew myself to be was gone, I was still fully aware. This awareness was watching the whole drama. The awareness was wise; it spoke the truth. I was one with it. When I realized this, I felt a profound calm I had never experienced before. That which I am is beyond life and death. All I could say was, 'I'm home, I'm home, I'm home.'"

"Amazing. A blessing." Knowing there were many more stories, I said, "Tell me more."

"In 1962, Tim Leary and I were staying at the Hotel Catalina in Zihuatanejo, Mexico, where we had created what Tim called a psychedelic summer camp and a glimpse of utopia, a six-week community of 'pioneers developing modern versions of the traditional techniques for philosophic inquiry and personal growth.'9 It was a wild season. The brochure called it a romantic hidden treasure in the sun. Tim called it Hotel Nirvana, the ultimate destination resort.

"One night I was swimming in the ocean. I had taken some LSD, and my mind was clear, the night spectacular. But I began to become disoriented by the lights reflected in the water, and I couldn't see the spotter—we always had a spotter, a ground control person, who would watch out for us when we tripped. I felt he had forgotten about me. The waves were big, and the surf began to seem wild, and I was right in them and could feel all the forces at play. I knew that if I was pulled under by one I might not be able to resurface because I didn't know which way was up. I wasn't sure whether I was going to come out of this one. I thought I might be drowning. But as I thought I might die, all I could think about were the social ripples of my death: close friends would come together to grieve, but then time would pass and the memory of me would slowly fade. I saw how a little girl might ask her mother, 'Who was Richard Alpert?' And her mother would have no idea. I didn't think of my own process—just what other people would think when I was gone. But then, without my doing anything, things began to change: I let go of my anxiety, and I saw my death as just a shift in the balance of nature, like a tree falling. I became just a part of the ocean, a transformation of energy. I thought I was dying, and it was all fine."

"What did you think when the trip was over?" I ask.

"I learned that the soul is not located in my body. I knew that when my body dies, awareness goes on."

After Maharaj-ji died, Ram Dass had another encounter with death on LSD. The unlikely setting for the story was a Midamerica hotel, in Salina, Kansas. He told us the story during the first summer of Naropa Institute (now Naropa University) in Boulder, Colorado, where he was lecturing to support Chögyam Trungpa Rinpoche's new educational venture.

I had been given some LSD, and Maharaj-ji had said I could take "the medicine" if I was alone in a cool place, feeling peace, and my heart was turned toward God. And all those conditions happened to be present at the Midamerica hotel. So I wrote out questions that I'd like to ask myself when I met me later, and I had a picture of Maharaj-ji taped over the television screen. I made it all beautiful with incense and candles, and I took off all my clothes and got nice and warm. Then I took the acid.

Well, it turned out to be stronger than I thought. I was told to take as much as would fit on the end of the matchstick, but I used a wooden match with a bigger tip. I am such a scientist! At some point, I realized that whatever was happening was too much, and I decided I was going to die. I rushed to the door to get the manager so he could call somebody to take me to a hospital, and I had my hand on the door when I saw the scenario about to play out: a naked, bald man in room 125 running around saying, 'Oh God! Oh God!' and 'Aw.' I decided of all the ways I could die this was not a desirable one.

So I came back into the room. I was desperately trying to find a way not to die, but everything I thought of ended in death. I began to panic. I finally caught sight of Maharaj-ji's image, and I said to him, 'There's no way out. I don't want to prolong it. I want to die. Please let me die now.' And I laid down to die. I saw my thoughts getting slower and slower and slower, until I saw each thought arising, existing, and passing away. And then I saw space between the thoughts, and I went into that space. And the next thought I had was, Well now, I can be anything I want next time around because the only thing that is going to die is the thought of who I am. And then the trip was over.

Now, after being with Maharaj-ji, learning to meditate, and reading the great teachings of Ramakrishna and others, there has developed in me a kind of calmness and presence, because I know that death is not an enemy.

THE ANTIDOTE TO FEAR IS LOVE

Later I ask, "If I'm not yet fully identified with the soul, and fearlessness doesn't come naturally, how do I stop feeling separate?"

"We can transform our separateness and invite the experience of interconnection through practicing compassion and love. The more we live in love, the more we see love everywhere we look. There is no separateness, and there is no fear. Remember, you can trust the unfolding. Enter into the flow of love with a quiet mind and see all things as part of yourself. This is the true freedom."

"Yes." I want to absorb that for a while.

Then Ram Dass continues, "Maharaj-ji said that it's all perfect. I take that to mean that even in suffering, even in dying, there is a place we can rest, not in fear but in love, with faith that it is all unfolding exactly as it should. I say that because I have deep faith in Maharaj-ji, and you do too, but we can also have faith in ourselves when we rest in the soul. We can have faith in our capacity for awareness and love, the place where the deepest truths are. That capacity in us isn't personal, it's universal. We all share it. We can trust those truths to guide us through life and into death.

"Maharaj-ji's teaching is love. The more open you are, the more you receive love. That love is with you wherever you are, even as you are dying. It's the beginning, the middle, and the end. It's the entrance to oneness. And it is available to everyone. As Frank Ostaseski said to me, 'Love is not a gated community. Everyone is allowed in.'"

This seems clear right now: it's about love as a way of being, not a feeling. The antidote to fear. It's always available, and it's limitless. Our friend Bob Shapiro had an insight at a retreat recently; he told me, "Love is viral. It's contagious." It's a public health issue.

Ram Dass says, "We all have the capacity to love. We grow into love through the familiar practices: be here now, learn to let go of attachments, cultivate compassion and lovingkindness, and die into loving awareness, over and over again. When lovingkindness practice feels too much like *doing* for me, then I rest in loving awareness. It's easier to stress the *being* part. Being love.

"If I change my identification from the ego to the soul, then, as I look at people, they all appear as souls to me. I change from my head—the thought of who I am—to my spiritual heart, feeling directly, intuiting, becoming loving awareness. It's a change from a worldly outer identification to a spiritual inner identification."

"How do you practice loving awareness?" I ask.

"Anyone can practice it, in any moment. Concentrate on your spiritual heart, right in the middle of your chest. Breathe in and out of your heart. Keep repeating the phrase, 'I am loving awareness. I am loving awareness. I am loving awareness.' When you and I rest together in this awareness, we swim together in the ocean of love. Remember, it's always right here. Enter into the flow of love with a quiet mind.

"I've realized that being love is the best preparation for death. Nowhere to go, nothing to fear, just loving awareness, unchanging, as everything around me changes, moment to moment. Being here right now, because immortality is in the moment, now and at the moment of death."

Now it's time for dinner. Something we love.

DEATH OVER YOUR SHOULDER

The next day, we are back in his room. It's quiet except for the sound of the workmen cleaning the gutters outside the window. "Gutter yoga," they call it.

Ram Dass jumps right into our subject. We had agreed to talk more about keeping death over our left shoulder, letting go of fear and denial, and how we get familiar with death. I tell him about a plumber I know who almost died from cancer. Now each time he says good-bye to someone, he imagines it is the last time so that he can be as loving as he wanted to be when he thought he was dying.

"That's good," says Ram Dass. "I once visited San Quentin, the men who were on death row."

Ram Dass tells me the story. He was invited to San Quentin, which Earl Smith, the prison chaplain and a friend of ours, has called "America's most menacing and frightening prison." San Quentin houses white- and blue-collar criminals, rapists, child predators, murderers, and serial killers. Built in 1852, the prison is in Marin County, just twelve miles north of San Francisco's Golden Gate Bridge.

When Ram Dass walked through the prison's iron gates, he was taken to death row, where most of the men were expected to die within sixty to ninety days. They led what looked like a bleak and dull existence. Ram Dass went up to each cage-like cell and shook hands "through the little food place." Out of some thirty-five men, all but about five received him "openly, clearly, quietly, consciously." He felt like he was visiting a monastery and these were the monks in their cells. These men were facing death. Their situation "cut through their melodrama, and they were right here."

After leading a meditation, sending out love and peace to all beings in the universe "direct from death row," Ram Dass became so moved that it was hard for him to leave. "There was light pouring out of their eyes."

Elisabeth Kübler-Ross, the psychiatrist who did pioneering work on death and grief, said to him later, "Ram Dass, we are all on death row." We just need to remember that. Their advantage is that they couldn't pretend they were not going to die, the way we do much of the time.

How do we stop pretending?

I told Ram Dass, "When Owen was two or three, we took him to the Jacques Marchais Museum of Tibetan Art on Staten Island. On the ferry ride back to Manhattan, we asked him how he liked it. That innocent little face looked at us and said one thing: 'The Buddha is not pretending.'"

How do we become the Buddha?

HELD IN MAUI'S ARMS

In the afternoon, Lei'ohu Ryder stops by, and while Ram Dass rests, she and I sit together outside, talking about Maui. Lei'ohu is a native Hawaiian and a spiritual leader, visionary, healer, singer-songwriter, and educator. Along with her partner, Maydeen 'Īao, she leads the opening and closing ceremonies for Ram Dass's retreats. I tell her that he and I are writing about death, which is an opening and a closing, and that I want her help to honor these conversations happening on the healing island of Maui.

Until Ram Dass moved there, I had not spent time on Maui, though I'd been to the other Hawaiian Islands. I had friends born and raised on O'ahu, and I led a retreat on the Big Island, at which Nainoa Thompson of the Polynesian Voyaging Society taught us about using the stars to navigate. I house-sat on Molokai once and loved the *Kupuna* hula at Hale Kealoha and the old-style music of Lono. But I didn't know much about Maui.

Lei'ohu settles into her chair on the lanai looking out at the garden. Her skin is sunny, and her brown hair curls softly. "He is being held in Maui's arms," she says. "Maui called him. It is a planetary portal, at Haleakalā. Ram Dass arrived just at the time my teacher and elder Aunty Mahilani Poepoe was dying. Since that time, Maui has been a sacred place for him. When I took him to the Kukuipuka Heiau, a temple and a doorway to the light, he cried. 'This is why I came to Maui,' he said.

"And with Ram Dass here, Maui has drawn his 'ohana together, the extended family, soul to soul. Everybody comes here to be with him, and the teaching of aloha [love, peace, compassion, interconnection] is in his energy and light. The energy can then go anywhere. The land, what we call 'āina, has fed him, so he can feed others."

"You know," I say, "we usually talk about how Maharaj-ji said to love everyone and serve everyone. But just as often, he said to love everyone and *feed* everyone."

"It's the same taproot, Mirabai," Lei'ohu says. "It's all the same. He is connected to the taproot of aloha. Maui strengthens his energy so he can reach people everywhere, and they can open up to love. Here he can feel the wind and hear nature speaking. And he can be safe in the ocean of aloha."

"He loves his weekly swims in the ocean."

"I've always directed him to look out at the sea. The family in the sea—the whales and turtles and fish—they are talking to him constantly," she says.

"Maui changes people," I say. "Ram Dass was always loving, but now he *is* love."

"Maui is the feminine spirit—it helps us unite and balance the male and female within ourselves. Here the stars are also a portal to what is beyond this world. A lot of communication comes through them."

"And what about this land the house is on?"

"There was a trail that led to the sea, which the community used. There were shrines to the deities, and fisher folk would fish here. The ancestors surround this house, blessing him."

FROM EGO TO SOUL

The next day, as I walk into his room, Ram Dass is lying back in his chair, looking out at the ocean of aloha. Kush the cat is stretched across his body. Ram Dass looks peaceful, yet he speaks immediately: "Dying is about moving from ego to soul, leaving the body and becoming the soul. I'm using the word *soul* in too many ways. You talk about the 'spiritual self'—you don't even use the word *soul*," he says to me. "When I use the word *soul* with other people, like Catholics and Buddhists, they tighten up."

"Well, Catholics do believe in souls, but maybe I know why some of them respond that way. I was a Catholic girl, went to Catholic schools from preschool through Georgetown graduate school. We studied the Baltimore Catechism, in which the first question was 'Why did God make me?' And the answer was 'God made me to know him, to love him, to serve him in this world, and to be happy with him in the next.'"

"Wow, wow! Know, love, and serve. Just like Maharaj-ji. That's pretty good," Ram Dass says.

"But being happy with him in the next world wasn't going to be easy. Our souls have to be pure when we die. The official Catholic definition of *soul* is that it is the spiritual principle of human beings. It doesn't die with the body but is reunited with the body in the final resurrection and then lives forever in either heaven or hell, depending on your sins.

"I remember the first picture in the catechism: three milk bottles—one empty and dark (original sin), one filled with milk (God's grace after baptism), and another with black spots in the white milk (sins). I always thought of my soul as a milk bottle, and I felt guilty about those spots."

Ram Dass is laughing.

"That may be why Catholics react when you talk about soul," I say, smiling, "but Buddhists?"

"As Buddhists, Sharon [Salzberg] and Joan [Halifax] give me a hard time. They won't say the word *soul*."

I have watched both Sharon and Joan tease Ram Dass about the soul. He and I have both studied with many Buddhist teachers, so we know that Buddhism says everything is impermanent, everything is interconnected, and all our actions have an effect on our future.

I say, "Buddhists don't believe there is any eternal, essential, and absolute something called a 'soul' or 'atman' at the core of all human beings and living creatures. But they believe we have essential nature, Buddha-nature, the 'awakeness' in which all good qualities reside."

"Sounds like that might be a soul."

"Well, it is if you think of it that way, if you try to identify yourself with it. But Buddha-nature is said to be empty of all concepts of self and identity as well as birth, death, time, space.

It's actually been called *anatman*, meaning 'no soul.' Why don't you tell me your own definition of *soul*?" I continue.

Ram Dass coughs. "Okay," he says. "That's good. I want to give these concepts to you. The individual soul is the *jivatman*, and the big soul, the supreme soul, is *atman*. Jivatman is finite and conditioned, while atman is infinite and eternal, the indestructible divine existence. It's also true that the atman includes God, guru, and self. As a soul, I am part of the atman, but also individual. I am identified with my soul, yet I am still a separate entity. The next step is for me to dive into the ocean, to become one with the All. At the end of life, my soul will fully merge with the atman and become one with it."

"Or," I say, "as Thomas Merton said, one thing's sure about heaven: there won't be much of *you* there!"

Ram Dass smiles and continues. "I am identifying with the soul, which comes directly from God. I love everything, but the universe is separate from me in my perception. The next step is giving up individuality. Death, you see, is the full transformation from identification with the ego ('Doctor, doctor, save me') to becoming one with the soul."

Ram Dass pauses as if he is listening to someone else and then says, "Wow!" He adds: "The soul takes its learning from the life just lived and goes on."

"Does it only merge with the atman when it's finished with all its incarnations?" I ask.

"Well, Maharaj-ji was merged with the atman in this life, and he was also a soul."

"How can we understand that?" I ask.

"Maharaj-ji's soul was merged with the atman, but he also had a body. We don't know whether Maharaj-ji had become enlightened in this lifetime or before. He was a Siddha yogi."

I say, "He could be a kind of a bodhisattva, choosing to come back until all beings are free from suffering. They say that Christ and the Buddha were like that, simultaneously existing at the level of duality and being one with all. Maybe we can't think of it in a linear or rational way. Maybe both are true at the same time. The Upanishads say that at death 'the soul becomes conscious and enters into Consciousness.'"

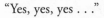

"Yes, yes, yes . . ."

"Okay, is this right? As a soul you merge with the Oneness after death, but you are still an individual soul until you finish your karma, finish needing to be an individual soul. And if you are finished, like Maharaj-ji, you have to hold both seamlessly."

Ram Dass: "Yes. And a person can slip into awareness of the One, even through psychedelics."

"I remember you used to tell us when we were tripping, 'Never forget your zip code, or you could fall off the mountain.'"

Ram Dass laughs again. "Maharaj-ji could hold both simultaneously, be in the One and be totally here talking about the price of potatoes. Wow!" Ram Dass says the word with genuine wonder in his voice.

"Some people say that was Steve Jobs's last word, *wow*," I say.

"Oh yeah, right!" Ram Dass replies, as he laughs and hits his thigh a few times.

THE EGO: SOMEBODY TRAINING

*T*he gutters are clean now, and the only sound from outside is the wind chime, shells tinkling against one another. We agree that it is important to be clear about the soul, because the essential teaching on dying is that the body and the ego die, but the soul does not.

"Ram Dass, I found a talk you gave on the soul and ego. I'll read it to you."

There is no inherent self—we are boundless. The ego is a structure of mind that organizes the universe, particularly around the relationship to separateness. It is in the domain of separateness. It is the steering mechanism for you as a separate entity surviving and functioning within the universe, within this world, on this plane. Then there's the other part of you that merges, that balances and flows and gives away everything and doesn't care, like the lilies in the field or the unconditional lover. And there's a tension between these two.

What happened to me as a soul was that I took birth into a good family, and they socialized me really well. They installed the software into my computer for the space suit I was wearing in this incarnation, which is called the ego. I developed a model of who I am, who you are, and how to function so that I could survive on this plane.

The predicament was that along the way I forgot I was a soul who had taken birth. I began to think that I was the computer program. For thirty years, I forgot who I was. I was busy being who I thought I was, who everybody had trained me to be. They trained me to be somebody, and the minute I got my "somebodiness" down, I went into "somebody special" training. I became somebody special, just like you did. You begin to take "yourself" seriously; you think you're real. That's the predicament most of us are stuck in most of the time.

It was Tim Leary, really, who began the change for me. He wanted me, as somebody he loved, to experience the psilocybin mushroom as he had, and I saw that I had another place to stand inside myself, from which I saw the game of Richard Alpert–ness. It was a beautiful game, but it wasn't who I was. I realized that who I was and who you are is far more interesting than the game we're playing. I was a soul. But I was still attached to my familiar way of being, and I kept falling back into the ego-centered view instead of a soul-centered view of reality. But as the Russian philosopher G. I. Gurdjieff said, "If you wish to escape from prison, the first thing you must realize is that you are in prison. If you think you're free, no escape is possible." I knew I wasn't free. I had seen everything from a different perspective. So I worked on getting a soul view. And that is what led me to Maharaj-ji.

Now, when you develop the ego, this central computer necessary for running the game, the problem is not the ego itself but how identified we are with it, as I was. In spiritual evolution, you don't destroy the ego; rather, you stop identifying with it. You see it as a functional unit. You need it to be functional so that, for example, when I'm talking to you, I realize there is a you and a me and we're talking on this plane. At the same time, if I am in touch with my soul, I know that I'm also just talking to myself.

The ego is a lousy master but a wonderful servant. The art is to convert that master into a servant. Ramakrishna talked about a horse-drawn carriage with a coachman sitting on top. The horses are desires, and the coachman is the ego. The coachman thinks he's handling the whole thing. But then the man inside the carriage, the awakening higher self, taps on the glass and says, "Turn left here," and the coachman says, "Who are you to tell me? What are you doing in there?" Higher self says, "I own the carriage, and you're my servant." And the ego says, "The hell you are!" Like, "I'm running this show. You need me to survive." It's not easy to train the ego.

The ego is not built on love. It's built on the fear of not surviving, and if that's who you think you are, then you're fearful all the time. And because you're fearful, you overcompensate and make decisions that further separate you from others and yourself.

The Sufis say, "You must live before you can die, but you must die before you can live." The dying that opens us to life is the letting go of our attachment to our desires and to the fruits of our actions—living life as it is, not as we want it to be; learning to simply be with what Aldous Huxley called "the miracle of naked existence," not trying to control what we can't control.

Ram Dass says, "Sounds good. Reminds me of when a retired editor of the *New York Times* wrote to me. He was starting a magazine called the *Obituary Quarterly*, where people could write their obituaries in advance of their death so that they could have them the way they would like them. A lot of people read the obituaries every day—I think because they are very real stories. He asked me to write my obituary, but I didn't really want to. It seemed a little . . . too cute. But after a while I did it. I said, 'Born, educated, father, mother, et cetera, colleges, books published'—you know, the whole routine. Then I wrote, 'About halfway through his life, he realized he had been going in the wrong direction. He had been busy becoming somebody, when the game in fact was to become nobody, nobody special, and the fact that this obituary is being published is proof that he failed.'"

I laugh. "Too good! George Orwell said that you wear a mask and then slowly but completely your face grows to fit it."

"Yup. That's what most of us do. But if you're lucky, you begin to hear what it means to be part of the Tao, or the flow, and you're nothing special, even when you're playing a special role, like I have at times. 'Ram Dass' will linger only a short time in memories."

Ram Dass pauses and then says, "'Ozymandias' . . ."

"The Shelley poem?" I ask.

"Yes," he says. "Somebody is walking out in the desert, barren desert, and he finds a big stone sticking up out of the ground with some writing on it. He clears it away and reads, 'I am Ozymandias, King of Kings; / Look on my Works, ye Mighty, and despair!'"

I say, "Ozymandias was somebody special—Ramses II, the most powerful pharaoh of Egypt—and that was all that was left."

SURRENDERING INTO THE ONE

We look at the ocean underneath the blue sky with its puffy white clouds. The ocean seems to have no distant shore, even though I know its waves are lapping or crashing on the beaches of Kodiak, Alaska, right now. In my mind, the ocean is the great Oneness, the atman, the big soul, which has no beginning and no end, no shores, no beaches, no map.

"The ocean helps me to surrender into the One," Ram Dass says. "Surrendering now, practicing surrender for when I really need it, for when it is a matter of life and death. I used to look at the ocean and feel content. It was great peace. Now the ocean is Oneness," he says. "That's what I see."

I tell him about a metaphor my friend Gopi Kallayil used when we were teaching together at the Sivananda Yoga Vedanta Center a month earlier. We were talking about yoga, how the word means "union," the union of individual consciousness with something bigger, with universal consciousness, the divine, the universe, atman. Gopi told us to think of ourselves as an ice cube, with our own cubic shape, white-blue color, cold temperature, and slippery texture—our iciness. We are pretty identified with being an ice cube, always at zero degrees centigrade. But if we're dropped into the ocean, our limited identity disappears as we merge into the vastness, becoming one with the sea, our iciness gone but our essence still there. We become part of the One.

"That's a good one," Ram Dass says.

Then he has to go to the bathroom and calls Lakshman on the intercom. Soon Lakshman lifts Ram Dass out of the armchair and into the wheelchair with a soft *thunk!* and wheels him to the bathroom. He is gone for about fifteen minutes. Thinking about how Ram Dass has had to surrender to being helped with even the most basic functions, I also look at the books on his shelves: *Infinite Vision, Awakening Joy, Women of Wisdom, Life before Life, Who Dies?* When Ram Dass returns, Lakshman puts his feet into hot water to soak.

I say, "I remember when I was recovering from a broken foot. It was so hard for me to ask for help. I remember lying there, looking at a vase of flowers across the room and wanting so much to rearrange them. It was a small, unimportant thing, but it was driving me crazy, and I couldn't bring myself to ask anyone to do it. It seemed like too much. So I just lay there, unhappily looking at the daisies."

"Oh I know, I know, I know," says Ram Dass.

AGING LIKE A TREE

Once he is settled, Ram Dass says, "This is how it is to be an old man. For anyone attached to self-image, it's hard. Anybody thinking about the past . . ." He stops and is quiet, maybe absorbing the truth of what he just said.

We sit in silence for a while.

"Should we include something about aging in the book?" I ask. "I know you wrote a lot about it in *Still Here*."

"Well, yesterday, when that reporter on the phone was interviewing me, my friend on the call helped me. I was looking for words, and she finished my sentence. In that moment, I saw myself as an old man. I very rarely think of myself as an old man. I more often think of myself as . . ."—Ram Dass's eyes grow brighter—"as fucking rad."

I am laughing hard. The day before, someone had told Ram Dass he was "fucking rad," and he had had to ask Lucian what it meant. I say, "Well, it's all true at once, I guess. We don't mind being an old soul, but being an old person, an old man—that's different!"

We both smile.

Ram Dass says, "It's freeing. Aging is freeing. Fewer attachments. I used to comb my hair,

concerned about my baldness. Now I comb my hair with levity. Who cares about baldness!" Ram Dass smiles a big, slow smile.

He continues, "You need to find a place to stand in relation to change where you are not frightened by it. Be with the changes, work with the changes, but at the same time, cultivate emptiness, spaciousness, awareness, and clarity. This is what the deep spiritual work of sadhana is about.

"The first stage of that is seeing yourself as a soul. You aren't your incarnation, and you aren't your body. Yeats said, 'An aged man is but a paltry thing . . . unless / Soul clap its hands and sing.' Pull yourself out of the identification with the body.

"We have grown up in such a materialistic society, instead of cultivating the quality of being. In the East, many spend their lives preparing for aging and death. In the West, we spend our lives denying aging and death. And it can be harder to practice when you are older. Die in the morning, so you don't have to die at night. Gandhi was uttering his mantra when he was shot. He was ready for what was next."

We are quiet for a while. Then, in a surprise turn, Ram Dass says, "I'm thinking about trees."

I blink myself back into the room.

He goes on: "Accepting the natural unfolding of the life of your body, that's different from feeling young or old . . . like a tree . . ."

We look out at the graceful palms, swaying their fronds, so many colors of green. They are not worried about aging.

I say, "One time E. J. picked me up at the airport after I'd been somewhere, maybe here, and I said, 'Oh, I'm so tired. I think I'm getting too old to travel so much.' And he said, '*Getting* old, Mirabai? You are not *getting* old, you *are* old!'"

We both laugh.

I share that I love Paul Simon's birthday song: "God is old. We're not old. God is old. He made the mold."

Ram Dass laughs. "It was strange for me when I knew that I was passing Maharaj-ji . . ."

"In earth years?"

"Yeah. That felt old."

I say, "You didn't age the way most people age. You were aged by the stroke, so the usual markers of age since then don't feel relevant. Dahlia says that you can tell people are old because they have crinkly skin and they are wiser. And you *are* wiser."

"I became a soul after the stroke. The stroke made me delve within. That was when I started a whole new perception. When it happened, I didn't understand at first that it was Maharaj-ji's grace. But as everyone around me in the hospital room was tsk-ing and worrying, I looked up at Maharaj-ji's picture and saw him smile and say, 'Wait and see.' I waited, and I saw. Now I'm waiting for death, and then I'll see . . ."

Lakshman comes to take Ram Dass's feet out of the water. "Good to let them dry out," he says. "I'll bring more hot water later." He dries off Ram Dass's feet and says, "The deed is done. You can go back to talking."

But we are ready for a break. Ram Dass lies back in his chair, his feet free. I gather up my notes and the recorder and walk down the stairs.

In the bathroom, I look in the mirror and see an aging face. Why don't people get more beautiful as they age? I know, I know, Georgia O'Keeffe did and Ella Fitzgerald did, but not most of us. So I take off my glasses, and amazingly, I look like I have the skin of a Botticelli Madonna. We manipulate our lives so we can see what we want to see. Hard to accept, but true. I look old because I am old, which means that I am going to die soon. It would be good to think about that more often. And to remember that this is not the face of my soul.

And it would also be good to apply a little more moisturizer.

SPEAK, MEMORY

I n my room, sipping tea, I think about aging some more. I ask myself what my fears of aging are. Nothing comes into my mind. I feel good. I am energetic. I don't like those deep wrinkles on my forehead, but I don't really care that much. But wait, what about forgetting? Not the big forgetting, like forgetting the experience of being born or seeing the world for the first time, but short-term forgetting—*Did I put Trudy's number in my iPhone or not? Where did I leave my sunglasses? Did I answer that invitation to teach at Esalen?*

It's pretty scary to lose a capacity that you always had; it's especially scary to forget something a minute or two after it happens. *Did I take that calcium?* I ask myself in the morning as I am taking my multivitamin. I tell myself it's early, and I'm still sleepy, and I haven't had my coffee yet. But did that happen when I was younger and sleepy? I don't think so—but I don't remember!

For a while, I was making excuses to myself. I'd tell myself I was thinking about who should teach the retreat for the army, so I didn't pay attention to where I put the keys. At home one night, I looked out my bedroom window and saw a light in the meditation room. Did I leave a candle burning? I couldn't remember. What if I did? Could the glass vigil light break and start a fire? I had just closed my Nigerian novel, was settling into a soft pillow, and didn't want to get up, go downstairs, put on shoes, go outside, and walk down the flagstone path, in through my office, and into the meditation room. But I did, and there was no candle!—only a tiny orange light on the battery for the invisible fence we had for our dog, Nadine. That was it. I walked back across the yard, turned out all the lights, got back in bed, and was wide awake.

Most of the forgetting isn't very serious. It's the free-floating fear that goes with it, the fear of forgetting really important things in the future, forgetting to turn off the burner on the stove, forgetting how to get home, forgetting who I am. In response, I am madly taking vitamins and supplements (when I remember) and doing yoga and aerobic exercise and keeping my brain working on projects, like a fund-raising letter for the Love Serve Remember Foundation, a conference for the Center for Contemplative Mind in Society, and something else—I can't remember! Oh, right, finding a math game for Dahlia and writing a talk on right livelihood. So much! No wonder I can't remember. I am still being Joan of Arc, saving the world—at seventy-seven. Maybe I should shift my allegiance to Mnemosyne, the goddess of memory and mother of Thalia (the goddess of comedy!).

I will not remember dying.

DEATH IS A MOMENT

The next day, Ram Dass asks Lucian to join us. Lucian is in his twenties and grew up in Colorado, his father an academic. I am glad he's with us. I am aware that Ram Dass and I have been thinking mainly about death coming in middle or old age, although we know it happens also to young and even very young people. I remember a time in the nineties when I was working on a project with Bill Moyers, a program on dying called *On Our Own Terms*. It was focused primarily on empowering the dying to choose where and how they die. With Frank Ostaseski, I was teaching the production crew some meditation techniques to help them encounter their own fears about death, since those fears were likely to arise as they filmed dying people in hospices. After a full day of meetings, I met my son, Owen, who was then a student at Tisch, the NYU film school, in the East Village for dinner.

I told him what we were working on, and he didn't seem very interested. "Well, what does dying mean to you?" I asked him. "AIDS, guns, and climate change," he said. An instant reframe! My implicit bias was revealed—it was a different world in your twenties in New York City, where even thoughts about the universal experience of death were very different from mine. One time in a bookstore near NYU, I overheard a student make the quintessential statement on the subject: "The thing about life is that one day you'll be dead." So I am happy to have the younger Lucian in the conversation.

He says, "Death is hard to think about because we know we will die but have no empirical data about what happens after death. We have people who have had near-death experiences, but nobody who has actually died. . . . One teacher talked about death yoga."

"What's that?" I asked. "Sounds like having to stay in Down Dog for an hour."

"It's about focusing on death, but my friend said he prefers tantra yoga instead—at least you have more than one shot!" There is that about death. No rehearsals. Just one shot. So it will be good to be ready.

Ram Dass says that maybe talking about death as we have been is, ironically, keeping him from being in the moment, the best preparation for death.

Lucian asks, "So how do I keep death present while leading a full life, being here and now, doing all my tasks?"

Before Ram Dass can answer, death comes into the moment: Lucian remembers the death of a childhood pet. At eight, he had a cat named Mewty. "One day my dad ran over Mewty's legs with his car. My parents took Mewty to the hospital, where the doctors put casts on his legs. They came home to tell me, and in the middle of the night, I made them take me back to the hospital. I was so worked up. I petted his little casted legs. I realized then that I loved him. But later, they had to put him down. It was tragic. It is still sad."

We all feel sad.

After a little mourning period for Mewty, Ram Dass says, "Death is a moment, and how you spend your life in each moment is the rehearsal for your death. It's called *be here now*. It's your thoughts just this moment . . . this moment . . . this moment. You delve into this moment—that's all there is. When you are living in time and letting the monkey of your mind run around into past and future, that's your mind. But here we are. And death will also be a moment.

"Death often comes without warning, but we can begin to understand it by realizing that the opposite of death isn't life, the opposite of death is birth. The beginning and the end are two sacred events, and in between it is all impermanent. Life is arising and slipping away, each moment, each breath. But within us is awareness. It's unconditioned and eternal.

"Anagarika Munindra once said to me, 'Every breath is the first and the last.'"

"Who was Anagarika Munindra?" Lucian asks.

I say, "He was a Bengali Vipassana meditation teacher we met when we were first in Bodh Gaya. He was close to Goenka. *Anagarika* means 'one who leads a nomadic life without attachment in order to focus on the dharma.'"

Ram Dass goes on: "We can see death as a gift. We don't usually see it this way, but awareness of death changes our lives fundamentally. It helps us know how to live. And as Yogananda said, there is a great paradox in death: it is an experience through which we are meant to learn the lesson that we cannot die."

"What does that mean, 'We can't die'?" Lucian asks.

"This body you live in and the ego that identifies with it are just like the old family car," Ram Dass answers. "They are functional entities in which your soul travels through your incarnation. But when they are used up, they die. The most graceful thing to do is just to allow them to die peacefully and naturally. After death, the soul will live on. Eventually, in some incarnation, when you've finished your work, your soul will merge back into the One . . . back into God . . . back into the atman, the Infinite. In the meantime, your soul is using bodies, egos, and personalities to work through the karma of each incarnation."

Lucian asks, "If the soul lives forever, why are we afraid of death?"

"The ego is built on the fear of not surviving, and if that's who you think you are, you're fearful. The ego asks, 'Why not live *for* the moment? Eat, drink, and be merry, for tomorrow you will die.' But if instead you live *in* the moment, being here now, discovering the preciousness of life in each moment, then you are living, not as an ego, but as a soul, outside time."

Lucian says, "I sort of get it, but . . ."

Ram Dass tells the story of the wild strawberry. "One day, while walking through the wilderness, a man stumbled upon a vicious tiger. He ran but soon came to the edge of a high cliff. He looked over the cliff, and there at the bottom was another tiger. Desperate to save himself, he saw a vine and climbed down the fatal precipice, looking for a place to hold on. As he hung there, two mice appeared from a hole in the cliff and began gnawing on the vine. Doomed! Suddenly, he noticed on the vine a plump, ripe, wild strawberry. He plucked it and popped it in his mouth. It was incredibly delicious!

"The man knew that he was about to die and that there was nothing he could do about it. The strawberry was his last chance to enjoy life, so instead of wasting his last moments in fear and frustration, he took what pleasure he could and made the best of it."

Ram Dass sips his tea for a while as we reflect on that story. It is the essence of being here now—both the story and the tea drinking.

Then he continues, "That's the whole predicament of living and dying. You are always, at every moment, between tigers and holding on to a vine that is being eaten away, and right here is always the strawberry and its sweetness. In the moment, there is only the taste of the strawberry. You can be enjoying the strawberry, unless you are busy being panicked about what just happened or what's going to happen.

"The secret of dying is the secret of living, which is to be in the present moment. At the moment of dying, if the pain is great and you are busy pushing it away, you will be totally preoccupied with the pain—or your fear of the unknown for yourself or your loved ones can get so great that you miss the known in the moment. All the preparation for dying is so that as the time of dying comes, you can say, like Aldous Huxley, 'My goodness, look at that! Extraordinary! Ah, the body is going—how interesting. And here we are. And here we are.'"

LOVE
EVERYONE

All the universe has come from love,
and unto love all things return.

TAITTIRIYA UPANISHAD

IT'S ALL ABOUT LOVE

This morning Ram Dass has a temperature of 100.3, and we are worried that his urinary tract infection may have returned. By afternoon he feels well enough for a visit, but he has to be lying down with his feet elevated. He has agreed to see two friends of mine from Silicon Valley who want to talk with him about making a difference in the world. When they arrive at his room, Ram Dass is supine, and my friends sit down in two chairs at the end of Ram Dass's lounger, near his raised feet. It's an odd setup, but Ram Dass welcomes them—and after a while, it begins to seem normal.

Together, they talk about the difference between doing and being. Both friends have been successful in the technology world, and both now have spiritual practices. Ram Dass tells the story of how *Be Here Now* became a book without his trying to make it happen: a teaching on letting go, having faith, and having fun.

"When I returned from India in the sixties, after meeting Maharaj-ji for the first time and learning to meditate and do yoga, people wanted to hear the story, so I gave a series of lectures in New York. Without my knowing, one of the attendees, Lillian North, a court stenographer, took shorthand notes and later typed them out. As I was leaving New York, she handed me a big stack of papers, saying, 'Here are your words.' I put the papers in the back of my car.

"Soon after that, I went to Esalen. When I arrived, I was given a room in a couple's house, and the guy who carried my bag to the house asked me about the transcript. He was a writer serving as a gardener at Esalen. I told him. He said he could organize and edit the work and recommend which stories were worth telling. I agreed.

"From there I went to the Lama Foundation, a spiritual commune near Taos, and my friend Steve [Nooruddeen] Durkee asked, 'What's that?' When I told him, he suggested that the community's residents edit, illustrate, and lay out the text. Later, six artists and I sat around a big table reading the stories. Each of them selected one to illustrate. The Lama Foundation published the first version as a set of booklets in a box; later a friend of Steve's, Bruce Harris, who worked for Crown Publishing, published these booklets in book form. Now, almost two million copies have been sold.

"I didn't do anything. Maharaj-ji did it all. Give your plans to Maharaj-ji. Let him do it."

My friends have other questions about what to do, how to serve: "If you had unlimited resources, what would you do to make the world a better place?"

I expect Ram Dass will talk about our experiences with the Seva Foundation, but he doesn't: "I'd keep just enough for myself and my family and my obligations, and, you know, old age, and I'd give away the rest. Then I'd use the time for sadhana. Whatever you do, who you are is what will make the difference. Learn to identify with your soul. Do it with love. It's all about love."

After my friends have been there about an hour, I think Ram Dass must be getting tired, although he doesn't look it. I ask him to lead a loving awareness meditation, and he does: "Breathe in and out, silently repeating, 'I am loving awareness.'" His voice is strong but very soft. "I am loving awareness. I am loving awareness." When it is over, he looks at each of them fully: "I love you. I love you. I love you," he says, drawing out the word *love*.

I walk my friends downstairs, and we hug. We are all in a slightly altered state. "That's who I want to be," says Bo. "Love you." "See you in California." They walk out into a rainstorm.

When I go upstairs, Ram Dass's cat, Kush, is on his lap again, pressing his paws one at a time into Ram Dass through the blanket. He reaches over to pet Kush.

We decide to talk about the relationship between love and death tomorrow.

LOVE IS MORE POWERFUL
THAN DEATH

Love is from the infinite, and will remain until eternity.
The seeker of love escapes the chains of birth and death.

RUMI

In the morning, Ram Dass is feeling good. I am, once again, amazed at his resilience. I say, "That was powerful yesterday. Great advice—becoming love."

"It's all about love. Maharaj-ji taught me, 'Ram Dass, love everyone. Tell the truth. Serve everyone. Be like Gandhi. Remember God.' As I got older, the words 'love everyone' became the most resonant. I keep experiencing how loving everyone and everything is what allows me to stay in my soul, where I have no desires most of the time. There I feel present with what is, and I am content with what is given.

"We are all one. We are all talking to ourselves when we talk to one another. There is the plane of the ego, the plane of the soul, and the plane of the One. As you go on, you gravitate toward the One. Compassion comes from that realization of our oneness. When another person is suffering, you are suffering. When you help that person, you are helping yourself. When you love that person, you are also loving yourself."

"Well, what do you think Maharaj-ji meant when he said that love is more powerful than death?" I ask.

"The body dies, the thinking mind dies, attachments fall away. But the deep love in the heart, the love of the soul, goes on. It's as if love and death are intimately entwined.

When someone you love dies, the love continues. You just have to meet each other in a new way. If you can practice resting in loving awareness, you will be able to meet soul to soul.

"A woman whose husband had died came to me wanting to contact him," Ram Dass continues. "I said to her, 'You have work to do: identify with the soul, your spiritual self, and then your loving thoughts will bring your husband to you, because he is loving you as a soul.' A few days later, she returned and said that I was right. It was the love between them that did it."

I tell Ram Dass that our friend Ramesh, whose young daughter was killed while riding her bike, has said, "When I can go into the quiet, I can be with her. It's the same with Maharaj-ji. How does that make life and death a continuum? It feels as if they interpenetrate, and love is a kind of bridge."

"Souls love each other," Ram Dass responds. "They contact each other from plane to plane. When Maharaj-ji died, the love just became greater. Maharaj-ji is the closest being in my life. He is the truth that I live with every day. When I went to India, I was looking for a map reader. Maharaj-ji didn't read the map—he *was* the map, and he was the territory. And the fact that he isn't in his form just makes me understand him in ways much more profound than I ever would have had he remained in his form. His form was something I could keep at a distance. The love where we meet now is something that is inside me . . . the trueness of the love we tasted.

"Maharaj-ji is my path and my practice. During our first meeting, I was sitting very close to him on the grass, and I was sensing that he knew my thoughts. I was embarrassed at this man knowing my thoughts. I thought of the things I didn't want him to know about me. And then I looked up into his eyes, and he was looking at me as I had never been looked at: he was looking with unconditional love. I had never experienced such love from anybody. Everyone else had wanted something from me—my parents, my teachers, my friends, everybody.

But here I was, being truly loved, with no conditions. That moment changed my life and is linked by a chain of love to this moment.

"Since then, he has been with me in many ways. At first, I thought of him as a great teacher in India who loved me as I had never been loved, but I was seeing him in an emotional way while basking in his love. I kept trying to turn him into a personality, but that didn't work. It interfered with the free flow of his love. Slowly, I began to see that his love was impersonal, yet unconditional, a greater love than I had at first imagined. He didn't love me more than others; he loved us all completely. He was an ocean of love.

"After he died, he became an invisible, loving companion to me. He was an imaginary inspiration and rascally playmate who still loved me unconditionally. I took walks with him. I had long conversations with him. He helped me see the world through the lens of love. Someone said to me, 'You talk to your guru—don't you know that's your imagination?' Yes, that's how he came to me, through imagination. Einstein said that imagination is more important than knowledge. Knowledge is limited to all we now know and understand, while imagination embraces the entire world and all there ever will be to know and understand.

"And then, as more time went by, I began to experience him more often as becoming one with me, not separate. There is a room in my consciousness where he and I meet. And there we are, hanging out together in love." Ram Dass is smiling, thinking about Maharaj-ji.

"Do you find now, as you are getting closer to your own dying, that Maharaj-ji is not only becoming one with you but present in a more intimate or vivid way? Is it changing?" I ask.

"Maharaj-ji is in Soul Land, and I am in Soul Land, and now Maharaj-ji beckons to me to merge with him. I'm not there yet. I am still longing to be one with him. I have to get rid of that part of my ego that keeps us apart. But I'm not in a rush, because the path is the goal. I'm a bhakti, and it's the path of love, of longing, of yearning for oneness. I'm finding it through becoming one with the clouds, the ocean, the wind, this moment . . .

"Maharaj-ji is like the North Star, always and forever there, like the clouds here, all revolving around Maui, but Maui stays the same."

By love he knows me in truth,
Who I am and what I am.
And when he knows me in truth, he enters into my Being.

BHAGAVAD GITA

LOSE YOURSELF IN LOVE

When we meet again, Ram Dass says, "Love brings things together into oneness. You can't reach for it. You have to *be* it.

"Love has no judgment. It is boundless. You are standing on the beach, you put down your shoes and your ego, and then you dive in.

"If we love well, we will die well. Making peace with death and being fully in the moment allows us to lose ourselves in love, in the love of the beauty and awe of the manifestation of God, in the love of ourselves and others, and in the love of everything else—the suffering, the pain, the joy. We can't know when we will die, and living without knowing requires surrender, surrendering our hope and fear so we can open our hearts to life and let compassion grow. Then when death comes, we are ready to go into love, into the Light, toward the One."

I say, "Maharaj-ji told me to 'never go where there is no love.' And he gave me the name Mirabai. It makes me happy."

A memory of a time when I was in Burma in the nineties arises in my mind. I turn on my computer, dig into the files, and read this journal entry to Ram Dass:

I spread my shawl on the floor of the cabin and sit on my inflatable zafu. I close my eyes and begin to do lovingkindness practice: breathing in and out of my heart, "May I be happy; may I be peaceful." I open my eyes and look at the picture of Maharaj-ji. He is sitting on a wood tucket, a table-like bed, wrapped in his plaid wool blanket, as he stares into vast space, and I am sitting on the ground, leaning toward him, arms on the tucket. He rarely spoke to us, and then usually in short phrases: "Love everyone." I had questions when I first arrived. It wasn't that they didn't get answered; it was more like they fell away. He had given me my name the week that picture was taken: Mirabai, the ecstatic. Mirabai was a princess in India in the sixteenth century who had fallen in love with God (in the form of Krishna known as Giridhar, the one who lifts mountains) and fearlessly left the palace and all her worldly possessions so she could compose love poetry and sing to him. She is known in Hinduism as the embodiment of erotic bhakti, loving God as your lover. She found freedom through love; as she put it, "Mira's love is half lion and half man. She turns her life over to the midnight of his hair."

In the Hindu tradition, when your guru gives you a name, your practice is to live into it, to be inspired by it, challenged and awakened by it. "Ram Dass" means servant of God. So my practice is to live as Mira did, but in some twenty-first century way to be "mad with love." "I praise the mountain energy night and day. I take the ecstatic path human beings have taken for centuries," said Mira. So here I am. Learning to be mad with love. Letting the other parts of me fall away. And loving God—it doesn't have to be theistic; it can be loving everything in the universe.

"That's beautiful," Ram Dass says. "It's the right name for you."

After a few minutes, he goes on: "Love is what we are. I now see everything with love. Someone visits me, and what I see is love. I talk to a tree, and the tree is love. The ocean is love. The carpet on my floor is love. And if I go into the place in my self that is love and you go into the place in your self that is love, we are together in love. No you. No I. *We* are *being* love. That's the entrance to oneness."

There is a lot of love in the room: Ram Dass, me, Maharaj-ji, Kush the cat. Maybe it's time to just enjoy it. I say, "Let's have some tea." We call on the intercom, and Lakshman brings up hot, steaming, fragrant mint tea. What a gift!

79

LOVE HEALS

Ram Dass says, "Love can break your heart, but it can also heal your heart. If it is not the time for physical healing, love heals us into another kind of wholeness."

"Yes," I say, remembering myself as a child. "My father broke my heart. He left when I was seven. I cried and cried. He could break it because I loved him so much. I didn't think it would ever be whole again, but when Maharaj-ji looked at me, I felt like he was loving me as if I were totally lovable, like I was the only person in the world. I felt whole, healed, loved completely. And everyone there felt that. Amazing."

"Love brings us together into oneness."

"But we both have experienced a lot of love that wasn't about oneness," I say. "Good at the beginning and then a struggle. Big neediness. Thinking that love is something given to us by others, which can be taken away. Remember all those lectures you gave about relationships?"

"Yes," Ram Dass answers. "That's because the love that we see celebrated most often in our society is not the love that connects us all. In our culture and in the media, most love is romantic love, conditional love—'true love,' 'love at first sight,' 'I love you, and you love me.' We see love as something waiting to be found and grasped or fallen into or out of. But the truth is, you can't get love *from* anybody or give love *to* anybody. You *are* love. Sometimes another person helps you realize that, or you help them—and that is a great experience."

Then we are both quiet until Ram Dass says, "Fear of loving another person, of not being loved back, of being vulnerable, rejected, abandoned—all of that is about holding on to who you think you are."

I respond, "The line between love and attachment is thin and hard to see. I think that a lot of times we don't allow ourselves to love because of fear—fear of being vulnerable, fear that people will not love us back, fear of seeming foolish, fear of being seen for who we are, fear of being left alone. We need to get over the fear, so we can love."

"Fear of a broken heart," Ram Dass says. The way he says it in that moment almost breaks my heart. My arms feel weak. We are quiet for a while.

Then he says, "In conventional relationships, the trap is attachment to things being a certain way, to our lover behaving in a certain way, and if things change, we become dissatisfied and fall out of love. We go through life a little bit like hungry ghosts. This is so deep within all of us. Everybody needs love, and we think that the more we get, the better, and that if we don't get it, we are deprived. In that sense, it's like an achievement. You know, people who are achievers—the minute they achieve something, it becomes irrelevant, and their awareness turns to achieving the next thing. The predicament with conditional love is that although it can open our heart to kindness and caring and gratitude, we can get so caught in a relationship that we don't learn how to dwell fully in unconditional love. When our lover leaves, we feel hungry again. We think it is hunger for that person, but it's actually the hunger to be at peace, to come home, to feel at one in the universe, where lover and beloved merge. It's the longing to live fully in the moment."

I start laughing. "I am trying to think of people who are hard for me to love." And then, laughing into the word *love*, I say, "I can't come up with anything."

"Well," says Ram Dass, "what about tax people, businesspeople, politicians?"

Donald Trump has just been elected president.

"You know, it's interesting." I say. "You remember how I hated the Guatemalan army, which had waged war against the Mayan farming villages in the mountains?"

"Of course."

"One time we were flying up to one of those little Guatemalan villages in the mountains, when we were accompanying the return of the refugees from Mexico. They had lost everything and were at last going to start rebuilding. It was a little plane—there were four of us. It wasn't a military plane, but most of the pilots were ex-military, like here. And I thought, *Oh my God! I am going up in this little plane with the dreaded Guatemalan military. Eek!* Oh—and everybody had to get weighed. I thought, *You are the only person in the world besides me who knows how much I weigh!*"

More laughter from Ram Dass.

"Then, to balance the plane, the three other people had to sit in the back, so I sat in the front next to the pilot. And it was so beautiful up in the clouds. You know since you used to fly your plane. It was so beautiful. And then the pilot turned to me and said, 'Want to fly?' I said, 'I can't fly!' 'Here, take the wheel. This is what you do.' And the pilot gave me about five minutes of instruction. 'I'll be right here,' he assured me. 'Go ahead.' And I flew the plane, and it was thrilling! I was thrilled to be alive and to be flying! And then the pilot brought it down, and I just threw my arms around him: 'Thank you so much! I loved that.'"

Ram Dass and I were both laughing.

"Oh God! I didn't forget the immoral, merciless army actions, but I was now also aware of the ways in which this pilot was a human being, just like me, who had just done a kind thing."

Ram Dass says, "The kind of love that is not dependent on conditions is conscious love, or unconditional love, or Christ's love, or God's love, *metta*, agape. Unconditional love exists in each one of us. We just need to slow down enough to let our minds come into harmony with our hearts. Love is boundless."

I reach for my notebook for the quotes I've been collecting for this conversation. "Bucky Fuller said, 'Love is omni-inclusive, progressively exquisite, understanding and tender and compassionately attuned to other than self.' The reception after his funeral was at our house in Cambridge. Do you remember? And this is interesting: he and his wife, after fifty years together, died within twenty-four hours of each other. Compassionately attuned.

"And here's a good quote from the Bhagavad Gita. Krishna tells Arjuna, 'Give me your mind and your heart, and you will come to me.' It's as if he is saying, 'Always think of me, always love me, and I will guide your heart and your actions.' If you follow the path of the heart, you let your love and devotion guide you. You let your thinking mind be balanced by your loving heart."

Looking at Ram Dass, I say, "Love is empowering. People want to be with you, Ram Dass, because you love them. And then they feel like they have new strength to go on with what they know they should be doing. I've heard so many people say that. It's empowering to be loved. I mean, look at what happened to you with Maharaj-ji."

"Yup."

"I mean, hundreds, no, millions of people have been drawn to what you say because Maharaj-ji loved you. Think about it: millions of people!"

"Well, yes, the people tuning in to our webcast this afternoon are reaching for something."

Oh yes, the webcast! At that moment, the sound guys walk in. "Time for a sound checkaroonie," one says.

"Better change your clothes," Ram Dass says to me, taking care that we do everything properly. He's right: after this conversation I could easily forget and show up in the old T-shirt I am wearing. "I'll wear flowers," he says. "A Hawaiian shirt."

I leave Ram Dass with the sound guys and glide down the stairs. Love empowers. Love prepares us to die. Love everyone. Change your clothes.

INTERCONNECTED BY LOVE

On the webcast, in his Hawaiian shirt, Ram Dass says, slowly, "You become immersed in an ocean of love. Maharaj-ji was a soul lost in love. That's what he was telling us. We start out identified with ego, thinking that we are our thoughts and sensations and desires and personality, but if we work at it, over time we come to know our spiritual self, the soul, the place of love. He was telling us to use the time leading to death, from this very moment until our last, to open into loving awareness, to deepen into love, to identify with the soul. When he was telling me to love everyone and tell the truth, he was telling me to stay in my soul. Resting in the soul, where we become loving awareness, we *serve* all those in our lives because we are all interconnected by love. We meet in what I call Soul Country or Soul Land. And Maharaj-ji said to remember that the soul never dies, that this world is impermanent, and that we have everything we need to die with ease. Death is completely safe. It is not something we should fear. Just keep opening your heart."

I don't know what will happen after death, but I like the idea of Soul Land. One time I found Dahlia on the beach making a cake in the sand. She said she was in Cake Land. Cake Land, Soul Land . . . we have choices about where we want to be.

After the webcast, we run out of words and even out of silence after a while, so Ram Dass decides to take a rest. I take a fresh coconut and a straw down to the pool. While swimming, I think about Ram Dass, who is slower and paler than he used to be and some days has trouble with his breathing. There is an empty space around him that he used to fill up physically—but he seems surrounded by light.

When I see him later, he says, "I watched you swimming."

"Oh," I say, "how was my swimming stroke?"

He pauses and then extends the pause. Finally he says, "Reliable."

May you always find me reliable, I think. *May my love be reliable.*

That night Ram Dass wants to watch a Japanese film, *Departures*, about a young cellist who trains for a new professional role as a *nōkanshi*, one who prepares the dead for burial. I think he is interested in the cello part because he used to play the cello, but the movie is really about death, grief, service, and ritual. I think as I watch this beautiful movie that I want that ritual for my body when I die.

I ask Ram Dass where he wants his ashes spread when the time comes, and he says, "In the ocean"—he looks out the window—"out there."

SWIMMING IN LOVE

nother day begins, and we are sitting at the breakfast table, although we have finished the oatmeal and mangoes and cleared away the dishes. Krishna Das is visiting, and we are having a conversation that started forty years ago in India. The opening this time is a letter written by Vivekananda, a disciple of Ramakrishna who spoke at the first World's Parliament of Religions in Chicago in 1893 and introduced Hinduism and Vedanta to the West. Krishna Das has recently read the letter, written when Vivekananda was near the end of his life. Krishna Das says he was moved by Vivekananda's wondering whether he was teaching and speaking as a way of supporting his ego, whether he was attached to his fame and his students' appreciation, whether that was actually keeping him from coming "face to face with God."

Ram Dass says he still worries about that. And Krishna Das has struggled with it for years.

Then Krishna Das says what we know but keep forgetting: "I saw that people who were attracted to me weren't really attracted to me at all. They wanted connection to that place of love that I also wanted to be connected to."

The place we had discovered through Maharaj-ji. So what to do? That's the essence of our forty-year conversation: When we were with Maharaj-ji, what was he telling us to do and to be? If there is a relationship between what we do in the world, our dharma, and what we need to learn before we die, what should we be doing now?

"It's all about love," Ram Dass says. "It's about becoming love. You start out with ego and become a soul. Maharaj-ji was a soul lost in love. That's what he was telling us." We are all quiet for a few minutes, and then Ram Dass adds, "Sadhana . . . spiritual practice. Your work is your practice. If it's not taking you into love, it's not right for you."

He asks me, "Mirabai, when you were teaching the US Army, how could that be about love? I'm teaching people who want to learn to be loving. That's why they come to me. But the army can't want that. They kill people."

Good question. I like teaching with Ram Dass. I like that people want to be more loving, but I have also taught corporate executives, ex-gang leaders in Chicago, and medics and chaplains in the US Army.

"Well," I say, "they came to me. I was totally surprised. And it hasn't been easy; I'm still trying to work it out. But I went back to the Gita. Arjuna is a warrior, but he has no real desire to kill people on the other side. They may be greedy for his land, but they are his cousins, and they have families just like he does. He is trembling, his hair is standing on end, his skin is burning, and his weapon is slipping out of his hands. When he asks Krishna for help, Krishna tells him that this is his duty, protecting his tribe. Arjuna needs to do it with nobility, with wisdom and compassion, and without attachment, all of which he'll learn from his sadhana.

"The biggest lesson I am learning," I continue, "is that it's all just us. These soldiers are facing hard questions. How do you act in war, where you are given permission to kill other humans? How do you resolve the mission of increasing peace through destruction? How do you balance personal fear and grief with the demands of leadership? They may be wearing camouflage, but they need mindfulness and lovingkindness—just like everyone does, and maybe more—so that they can do their job consciously, be in the moment, and make wise decisions. They call it 'situational awareness,' and many of them respond to these practices with openness, kindness, care. They understand suffering—they are living on the knife-edge of life and death."

We are quiet again as the last word hangs in the air.

And then Ram Dass says, slowly, "Death." And after some time, "The difference and sameness of sadhana and death—they start out in ego and end in soul.

"Fear is the problem, and the root of fear is separateness. We transform separateness through compassion and love. So fear is an invitation to engage in practice and to be more loving."

There it was again. So simple: the answer to what we should be doing and how to avoid attachment to it before we die—or as we are dying. We have gone from oatmeal and mangoes to love and death in a very short time. Sadhana and love are the answer.

We all drop into silence. We had said we'd go for a swim, but we sit there and sit there and sit there, held by the silence. The sun is shining through the big Hawaiian windows, and a gecko is making the only sound.

After an hour or so, someone says, "We were going to go swimming."

We are swimming, I think.

DIE WITHOUT REGRETS

The next day at breakfast, Dassi tells us there is an email from Suzanne Gilbert asking Ram Dass to write or say a few lines for a collective tribute to our Seva Foundation friend Alejandra Álvarez. She died a few days before in San Cristóbal de las Casas, Mexico. As we age, so many of our friends are dying.

Ram Dass has had a hard night—pain, apparently from an implanted antibiotic, and not much sleep. But he gets fully into the tribute. He closes his eyes and drops into a space, quiet for a long time, and then he says softly, "Alejandra."

Alejandra. I could see her smile and her dark hair. We met in the mideighties, and she introduced us to the mysteries of Mexico and Guatemala. Ram Dass and my son, Owen, and I climbed the pyramid at Palenque in southern Mexico and took refuge from the rain in the Temple of the Jaguar. In Guatemala, she bore witness to that time of sad stories and beautiful weaving and introduced us to the cornstalk houses; the traumatized widows; the guy who told her that the village's truckload of fertilizer had been stolen; the shaman's son, who thought his tamales were being poisoned by a rival; the army coming through the village carrying AK-47s and terrifying the sweet, malnourished kids; the playful goats; the hope and wonder of the Mayan people; and, at don Vicente's hut, the *costumbre* wherein he prayed for the corn and the beans and us.

Ram Dass is quiet again, and then he says, "Her life was service with joy and a sense of humor and love for the people she served. She was a very here-and-now colleague. She stirred my heart for the project. It was always hard to leave anyone behind when she was involved.

Her life helped her understand the people she served." He pauses. "She was sparkly." Another pause. "She was more than a colleague." Pause. "She was a friend."

She would have loved to hear those words from Ram Dass, especially "sparkly." I don't think he had ever called her sparkly. I hope she hears it now, listening from wherever she is.

I think, *I'm going to start telling people more often what it is I love about them so they can hear it while they are living. I'm changing my to-do list from the tasks I faithfully work through every week to "tell friends what I love about them; die without regrets."*

RAM DASS REMEMBERS THE DEATHS OF LOVED ONES

You can't take away death,
but you can be there in love and comfort.

RAM DASS

ALDOUS HUXLEY

I first met the philosopher and writer Aldous Huxley, author of *The Perennial Philosophy*, *Brave New World*, and *The Doors of Perception*, while I was still at Harvard, where he participated in a psilocybin research session. In 1961, he, Tim, and I spoke at the Fourteenth Annual Congress of Applied Psychology in Copenhagen. Aldous spoke about visionary experience. Tim and I shook up the audience by saying that LSD and psilocybin could produce genuine mystical experience. Some scholars there said we had set back Danish psychology by twenty years.

Later Aldous gave us a copy of *The Tibetan Book of the Dead*, which mirrored much of my experience of dying on psychedelics and began changing my understanding of death.

In his novel *Island*, Aldous wrote about the death of the character Lakshmi, who died "dancing so lightly" into "luminous bliss," guided by her loving husband and friends through a process of letting go: "So now you can let go, my darling. . . . Let go. . . . Let go of this poor old body. You don't need it anymore. Let it fall away from you. Leave it lying there like a pile of worn-out clothes. . . . Go on, my darling, go on into the Light, into the peace, into the living peace of the Clear Light."[10]

Aldous actually wrote that as a blueprint for his own death, because even as he was finishing the manuscript, he was suffering from cancer of the throat. When it came time for him to die, he and his wife, Laura, took LSD together. She read the words from *Island*, but Aldous couldn't speak, so he wrote on a piece of paper, "Now I have lost the sensation in my toes, now in my legs, now my thighs." As he watched himself leave his body, there was no panic, no pushing death away. Aldous looked at the universe as an incredible manifestation of the divine law of creation, and at the end, he had just one word: "Extraordinary! Extraooordinary!" Because he was so accepting, such a dispassionate observer, he saw the divine law manifested in everything, including his own death.

MARAJ-JI

n September 1973, I was staying at my father's farm in New Hampshire when the telegram arrived. I had returned from shopping in the village, and my father and stepmother, looking rather concerned, met me. Dad said, "This telegram just came from India. I don't understand it, but I copied it down word for word as the operator gave it to me: 'At 1:15, September 11, Babaji left his bojhay [*sic*] in Vrindavan.'" The telegram went on with further details. "What does it mean?" my father asked.

Bo-jay? It took a minute. *Body?* "It means," I said, "that Maharaj-ji died."

Later I learn the story: On Maharaj-ji's final day at his temple in Kainchi, he sat with devotees, who sang devotional songs, and met with the "mothers," who cared for him. He visited each of the small temples on the grounds. He seemed agitated. His blanket was falling off, and when someone tried to fix it, he said, "Stop that. It's useless. I'm leaving central jail."

He had been complaining of problems and wanted to see a heart specialist in Agra. He asked Ravi Khanna, a young Indian devotee, to travel with him on the train to see the doctor.

They were joined by Dharm Narayan, Maharaj-ji's son. On the way back from Agra, the train stopped at Mathura, and Maharaj-ji decided to get off there. He was sweating and seemed cold, so they took him to the Ramakrishna Mission Sevashrama hospital, where he was attached to an oxygen tube that Maharaj-ji kept pulling out, saying, "*Bekar!*," which means "useless." He chanted *Jaya Jagadish Hare* (Hail to the Lord of the Universe) and passed away before the doctor got there. Maharaj-ji's body was laid on ice and cremated on a funeral pyre at the ashram in Vrindavan.

After I told my parents what the telegram meant, they immediately tried to console me, but their words seemed strangely irrelevant. I felt absolutely nothing, neither sad nor happy. There was no sense of loss. Perhaps I was just numb.

A couple with marital difficulties was waiting to see me, so I sat with them and helped them unwind the tangle of their love and hatred. Every now and then, in the midst of the discussion, my mind would wander, and I'd think, *Maharaj-ji isn't in his body. Isn't that strange? I wonder what will happen now.* But I pushed such thoughts aside and forced my back to the task at hand. Whatever was to come, there was no sense in stopping my service to others. After all, where could Maharaj-ji go? I knew he was in my heart. I had been living with him without his physical presence, moment by moment, there in New Hampshire, so did it really make any difference? Actually, I wasn't sure.

When the couple left, I started calling devotees in the United States and Canada and asking them to call others. Those within a radius of three or four hundred miles decided to join me in New Hampshire. By the next day, some twenty of us were gathered. It was a peculiar meeting. We were all dumbfounded by the news, and many were crying—but at the same time we were happy to be together and felt Maharaj-ji's presence very strongly. We cooked a big meal to eat around the fire, but before we ate, we went up to my room to sit at the puja table to meditate and sing to Maharaj-ji.

While we sang an ancient Sanskrit prayer, we took turns offering light to Maharaj-ji by waving a candle flame in front of his picture. After my turn, I went to the back of the group and watched the faces of my guru sisters and brothers in the reflection of the candlelight. Some were holding toddlers Maharaj-ji had named. I saw in their expressions the love and purity of their hearts, and finally I was able to cry—not at the sadness of the loss but at the presence of pure and perfect love that Maharaj-ji had awakened in us, which I felt in this gathering of hearts. "Love everyone," he had said, and at that moment I did.

Maharaj-ji is the closest being in my life. He is a living truth that I am with every day, and the fact that he isn't in his human form just makes me understand him in ways more profound than I could have had he remained in his form. The love where we meet now is formless inside of me. When Krishna Das asked an Indian devotee how to get closer to Maharaj-ji after his death, the devotee responded, "What are you talking about? Your guru is looking out of your eyes right now. That's where Maharaj-ji is." And that's how I know it to be.

TIMOTHY LEARY

Tim's dying and death in 1996 challenged many of the norms of our society. He turned his death into a theater piece, a dance, a celebratory moment. In 2014 my friend Gay Dillingham made a film about Tim called *Dying to Know*, narrated by Robert Redford, which centers on conversations Tim and I had before he died of cancer. The film begins with a resonant voice-over that recalls the early days: "Turn on, tune in, and drop out. Two Harvard professors. One ended up in jail, the other, a renowned spiritual teacher. They explored the edges of consciousness. They ended the fifties."

When Peggy Hitchcock, a good friend of Tim's and mine, is interviewed, she says, "Everyone's afraid to die. It's how we deal with it that counts. All the major social issues concern death." Then we see a younger me on-screen, and I say, "We have to allow the mystery of the universe to be awesome. If you love the universe, you become united with it. We have to create the right space for people to be less frightened. If you go into yourself deeply enough, truth is there. Life and death are one."

In a scene where Tim and I are hanging out in his room, you see psychedelic posters on the wall, a painting of the brain, another of the Buddha, and the two of us, looking like the old friends that we were. I ask Tim, "Who am I to you?," and he says, "Soul mate. Good friend."

"We are a dying breed, we say."

"I'm looking forward to the most fascinating experience in life: dying," Tim says. "I've been writing about self-directed dying for twenty years. You've got to approach your dying the way you live your life, with curiosity, with hope, with fascination, with courage, and with the help of your friends. I am determined to give death a better name—or die trying. You've got to take charge of it, plan it, talk to your friends about it."

When I ask Tim what he's learned from his investigation into death, he says, "I'm a good boy—a very good boy."

After watching the film recently, a group of us talked about Tim. When he started to die, he called me and said, "I've got great news, Richard!" "What's that?" I asked him. He said, "I've got cancer metastasized through my whole body, and I'm going to die. I feel like I just embarked on one of the most interesting adventures of my life." So I said to him, "Great, Timothy! Wonderful!" and I started to visit him. When I visited the first time, he was uploading video of himself onto his website. He said, "If you're information, that's what you do; you leave your information behind." And that was Timothy.

Tim was a romantic Irish bard. He and I didn't agree on the nature of soul and consciousness. Tim was a philosophical materialist. He didn't have a sense of the continuity of awareness beyond the brain and would never concur that we have souls—"I don't have that," he would say simply—nor did he believe there was an afterlife. But he did think he might be able to come back if scientists develop methods in the future, so he considered freezing his brain, but he finally decided to be cremated, planning what he called "the barbecue."

What Tim and I did share was history—our time at Harvard, me as the best man at his wedding to Nena while Miles Davis played, hours of cosmic adventuring on LSD, and love. We loved each other, and we had a sense of humor about it all.

While he was dying, Tim hosted a continuing salon, every day from noon to midnight, with movie actors and producers and mystics and philosophers and hippies and virtual-reality nerds all pouring through the house. "I'm going to die as a celebratory act," he said. "I'm going to use medication to reduce my pain and to enhance my clarity and my joy." And that's what he did.

As he drew nearer to his death, Tim and I started to look into each other's eyes. What I saw when I looked into his eyes was not somebody who was being clever about the theater piece he was doing; I met a being who was doing the dance but who was also behind the dance—and I had such a sense of "Go, dear friend, fellow adventurer. Go!"

At one point during his dying, Tim spoke the words "Why not?" He uttered the phrase repeatedly, in different intonations—as a question, as a statement, softly, loudly, thoughtfully, ruefully, confidently. He died soon after. Why not?

Tim died in his own bed, surrounded by friends and family. His son Zach said that until the end Tim was "maintaining his rascal quality" and that "the process of slipping into the unknown was very peaceful for Tim." After a festive wake, his body was cremated, and the ashes were divided among his loved ones.

His longtime friend John Perry Barlow wrote: "Timothy Leary died unashamed and having, as usual, a great time. He made good on his promise to give death a better name or to die trying. Willingly, peacefully, and unafraid, he headed off on his last trip."

After he died, reporters asked me, "How do you feel about the loss of Tim Leary?," and I said, "What loss? He's still with me."

Seven grams of Tim's ashes were buried in space, aboard a rocket carrying the remains of twenty-four others, including Gene Roddenberry (the creator of *Star Trek*), Gerard O'Neill (a space physicist), and Krafft Ehricke (a rocket scientist). A Pegasus rocket containing their remains launched on April 21, 1997, and remained in orbit for six years, until it burned up in the atmosphere. In 2015, the actress Susan Sarandon, a good friend of Tim's, put some of his ashes into an art installation at the Burning Man festival, where they were burned along with the installation.

MY FATHER, GEORGE ALPERT

ot everyone is ready to talk about dying—Tim was an exceptional case. We have to honor individual choices about when to open the subject. My father never wanted to talk about death. When he was about to have a minor surgery—though no operation is minor when you're eighty years old—I visited him in the hospital. We had a nice visit. I had my jacket on and was halfway out the door when Dad called me back: "Just in case things go wrong, is there anything I should know?"

I went back to his bedside and said, "All I can tell you is, as good as this is, that is going to be better. And wherever you go, I'll be there."

Dad said, "Great! That's all I wanted to know. See you later."

I took care of him for ten years after that. The last few years, we were in bliss together, which I think would have been true even if he hadn't been dying. He had been a great bear of a man, a high achiever, preoccupied with upward mobility for himself and his family. But as he got older, he started to let go of his need for power and control, and when he was very old, he let go more and more, until he was just a silent, smiling Buddha, an angel. In the past, when he was the president of the New York, New Haven and Hartford Railroad and first chairman of the Brandeis University Board of Trustees, we'd smoke cigars together and drink brandy, but we never held hands and watched the sunset. In those final years, though, I used to massage him and hold him and talk to him, and we'd look at the sunset together and hold hands.

One day, my brother Billy came to see him. My brother had always had difficulty with my father. That day he said, "Hi, Dad," and Dad just smiled his Buddha smile at him, the silent smile I had come to love. My brother walked out and said, "Stinker! He still won't talk to me." When my aunt, Dad's little sister, who loved my father immensely, visited, she asked him, "George, how are you?" He just smiled again. She said, "Oh George, what have they done to you? You're gone! You're gone!" They were troubled and angry because Dad wasn't who he used to be, but he was nicer than he'd ever been. And he and I were in bliss.

Dad died quietly. They took him away in a body bag. I was there. I think experiencing a parent's death is a liberating process, like becoming an adult in the spiritual sense.

MY STEPMOTHER, PHYLLIS HERSEY ALPERT

My stepmother, Phyllis, was a tough New England lady. She was a good woman, grounded, who played poker and smoked—just wonderful fun. She was also argumentative and willful and had a stiff-upper-lip way of living life, even when facing her death.

I didn't say, "Now let me instruct you about dying," because she would not have accepted that. I let her ask me whatever she wanted to ask. There came a moment when she gave up,

she surrendered, and it was like watching an egg breaking open and seeing a radiantly beautiful being emerge. She was clear and present and joyful. Always, at some level, she had known herself to be this being, but she had been too busy all her adult life to recognize it. Now she opened to this beautiful being in her core, and she basked in the radiance.

At that moment, she and I were completely together, just being. The whole process of dying was a series of moments of phenomena that were occurring. She was no longer busy dying. She was just being, and dying was happening.

Right at the last moment, she said, "Richard, sit me up." So I sat her up and put her legs over the edge of the bed. Her body was falling forward, so I put my hand on her chest. Then her body fell back, so I put my other hand on her back. Her head was lolling around, and I put my head against her head. We were just sitting there together. She took three breaths, three really deep breaths, and she left.

Now, if you read *The Tibetan Book of the Dead*, you will find that when conscious lamas leave their bodies, they sit up, take three deep breaths, and then leave. So who was my stepmother?

We held her memorial service at the Vedanta Centre in Cohasset, Massachusetts. In the program for her service, we printed these lines inspired by a verse from Rainer Maria Rilke:

in the sky the starry nights of another,
sweeter country blossom above her and will never close.

JEAN YEOMANS

Jean was a beautiful Quaker woman. I visited her when she was dying, and she said, "Oh, Ram Dass, I want you to help me die. I've had enough."

I said, "Jean, what's your rush? I mean, you know, you haven't lost your hearing yet . . . you haven't lost your sight. It's a precious birth."

She said, "Ram Dass, I'm so bored."

And I said, "Well, you're probably bored because you're busy dying all day. I mean, couldn't you die like ten minutes an hour? Do you have to die every minute? Dying is such a big drama. You are saying, 'I'm dying!' And then everybody says, 'She's dying!' And then it becomes: 'You're dying. Are you dying today? How are you dying? Are you dying well? Here's a counselor for dying. Here's . . .' and it is just something you happen to be doing. I mean, we're all dying, and we're not busy going around dying. Everybody we know will be dead within about seventy years."

She said, "I feel so closed in. The shades are too much, the light is too much, the sounds are too much."

I said, "Well, Jean, that's because you're trying to pour so much into such a small container. What do you say we expand together?"

So we held hands and closed our eyes, and I said, "Do you hear my voice? Let it be inside you. Hear the clock on the mantelpiece? Let it be inside you. Do you hear the kids playing out in the street? Let them be inside you instead of outside." And we just kept expanding and expanding and expanding. And there was a smile on her face, and she sat up and kissed me.

I said, "Well, now you know what I know. Have a good death." And I left, and she died a few hours later, with her husband by her bedside.

GINNY PFEIFFER

Ginny was an old friend and sister-in-law of Ernest Hemingway. She had lived in Paris and Spain, in circles that included Gertrude Stein and others. She was a friend of Laura Huxley for many years before Laura and Aldous married, and she lived with the Huxleys until she died. They were family together. When she died of pelvic cancer, she was still Hemingwayesque—cynical, intellectual, very hip, and beautiful.

When Ginny began to die, Laura and I and a very good doctor were with her. The four of us would sit around sharing the process of what her treatment should be: how much intravenous feeding she needed, what kind of drugs she should take to kill the pain, et cetera. And as she got weaker and weaker, I found that the most powerful thing I could do was just sit by her bedside and silently meditate on her crumbling body. I felt deep sadness watching her, knowing I couldn't take away all her pain, but my rocklike silence seemed to give her what she needed. She turned to me and whispered, "I'm feeling so much peace. I wouldn't be in any other place in the universe than here in this moment." I felt the same way. We had made space for truth to enter the room. She died soon after that.

DR. GOVINDAPPA VENKATASWAMY

first met Dr. Venkataswamy, whom we all knew as Dr. V, at a Seva Foundation meeting. We were all trying to be karma yogis, and then a real one came along. Dr. V had been a budding doctor when arthritis took hold, and then, with crippled fingers, he became an eye surgeon. He saw the arthritis as grace, and his example helped me to see my stroke as fierce grace. He affected so many people. Your life would be going in one direction, and then you'd meet him, and it would go in another direction. When I was with him, my potential through his eyes, my soul, was clear. Nobody else except Maharaj-ji treated me that way. My personality would push away my spiritual role, but Dr. V reinforced that role by treating me as a soul.

I have a feeling that Sri Aurobindo, Dr. V's guru, ran his life, just like Maharaj-ji runs mine. Dr. V could not have had the success he had on his own. He worked a miracle in the world of blindness, performing one hundred thousand sight-restoring operations with crippled fingers and establishing the Aravind Eye Care System, the largest and most productive eye-care system on the planet, now imitated around the world. He had a vision from another level. Even when everybody knew what a situation called for, he would hear a message offscreen that we should do it a different way. He was dancing to a different drummer.

In the late eighties and nineties, Dr. V began to have premonitions of death. He wrote in his journal about "a feeling that all men come like a maize crop, and all will pass from this earth in the course of time, and new people will come. Death is around the corner. Soul is eternal, with birth and death as different doors." In 2006, at eighty-eight years of age, Dr. V died at the Aravind Eye Hospital in Madurai. Pictures of Sri Aurobindo and his spiritual collaborator, the Mother, were pinned to the curtains in his room—the Mother's palms folded upward in the *namaste* position, Sri Aurobindo's expression more serious—and there was incense burning.

On his last days, his grandnieces read to him from Aurobindo: "When mind is still, then truth gets her chance to be heard in the purity of the silence. Death is but a changing of our robes, to wait in wedding garments at the Eternal's gate."

Close to the time of Dr. V's death, the room filled with nearly forty people, including his beloved sister Natchiar, many members of his extended family, and others from the hospital. He was quite peaceful, then his breathing became labored, quickened suddenly, and then a hush, stillness. A little while later, Natchiar's husband, Nam, reached over and gently closed the eyes of one who had had such deep vision.

CROSSING OVER

What looks like falling can largely be
experienced as falling upward and onward,
into a broader and deeper world,
where the soul has found its fullness
and is finally connected to the whole.

RICHARD ROHR

FORGIVENESS

I walk into Ram Dass's room and find him in his chair with his eyes closed. I sit down in my chair, turn on the recorder, and sip my chai. It is hot today, and there is not much of a breeze.

When Ram Dass opens his eyes, he says, "I was visualizing my death."

"Oh. Good practice. If you were to really die right now, would you be ready?" I ask him.

"Yeah," he says with what looks like a satisfied smile.

I wonder if I can say that—and mean it.

"Don't you have any regrets? Or people to forgive? Or anything unfinished?"

"I have a difficult time relating to regrets," Ram Dass tells me. "They are psychological. But I might regret not being able to be a vehicle for Maharaj-ji's teachings anymore."

"I like what you said before," I respond, "about allowing the past to arise and just loving it as it was and is now, and letting go, letting regrets fall away. For example, you said your mother did her best when you were a baby, so if you just love that memory for what it is, regret falls away.

"I hadn't thought much about regrets until my sister was dying," I go on, "but toward the end, she expressed regrets. 'I wasn't a good enough mother. I wasn't a good enough daughter.' Since she had dementia, she couldn't use her mind to tell herself otherwise. Her body was restless and almost writhing in her bed. She couldn't relax. We would tell her, 'I love you. You were a wonderful mother. You have wonderful children.' Her body began to relax and fall deeper into the bed as the love replaced the regrets."

"Yeah. Love is more powerful."

"Sometimes people need to actively forgive themselves or others before they can let go and be present. Nelson Mandela said that if you can't forgive, you can't heal. He said that as he walked out the door of his cell, free at last after twenty-seven years, he knew that if he didn't leave his bitterness and hatred behind, he'd still be in prison."

"That's it: the prison of your own mind," Ram Dass agrees. "The person I most forgive is my mother. The night before my first visit with Maharaj-ji, when I was remembering her, was the first time I saw her as a soul. The next day, Maharaj-ji said, 'She is a great soul.' I asked the translator, 'Didn't he say she *was* a great soul, because she is dead now?' And Maharaj-ji said, '*Nahin!! Nahin!*' No! He was seeing her as a soul, and I was remembering her as an ego. Since that moment when he said, '*Nahin,*' I see her as a soul who took birth, this time, as my mother.

"One of my doctors plays the didgeridoo. He plays it for me, and I find the sound takes me to other realms. In one of those sessions, my mother came to me and said, 'I'm proud of you. Don't mind the past.' That was a big thing for me, a Jewish boy. At her funeral, her dear friend had said to me, 'You should be ashamed of yourself. You caused your mother heartache.' It was hard not to believe that then. Now she was telling me that she forgives me." Ram Das laughs a little laugh: "Yum, yum."

"Oh, imagine saying that to someone at his mother's funeral," I say.

Ram Dass laughs hard. "Oh boy, oh boy." And then he says, "Now I forgive Mother, and Mother forgives me, and we love each other."

ON THE EDGE OF THE MYSTERY

This afternoon, I sit next to Ram Dass as he is Skyped into an auditorium of a thousand people at the Wisdom 2.0 Conference in San Francisco. The conference brings together technology executives and dharma teachers to talk about how meditation and yoga can create a more mindful and compassionate workplace, as well as how compassionate engineers can create technology that supports a more conscious life.

This session with Ram Dass is called "Death as an Advisor to Life." On stage are the Buddhist teachers Frank Ostaseski and Joan Halifax, both pioneers in end-of-life care, and the facilitator, Vanessa Callison-Burch, who is a product manager at Facebook, where they recently added a feature to the site that allows you to designate a "legacy contact" to manage your Facebook page after you die. Facebook is already a virtual cemetery of more than three million memorial sites. You never quite die if you're on the Internet. You are there for all eternity, or until the next technology comes along.

On the screen, Frank asks, "Ram Dass, what's it like coming close to death for you?"

"Well, for one thing, I'm becoming aware that many of the people who were my colleagues on this subject have died—Stephen Levine, Wayne Dyer, Elisabeth Kübler-Ross. Sometimes I feel like I'm flying alone. It's strange."

There is a long pause.

Then Frank says, "Life and death are a package deal. But we have overprofessionalized death and forgotten how natural it is. We have turned an intimate experience into a technological phenomenon. We have forgotten what we know: we can trust in our ability to do this, to accompany each other. When I die, I want the three *M*'s: someone with **mastery** around pain management, someone from the territory of **meaning** who has had real life experience, and also someone from the territory of **mystery**, the places we have never been before. But they may not all be available. How do we develop our hearts and minds so that if they are not there, we'll still be okay?"

"That's the role of sadhana," says Ram Dass. "Even a practice as simple as noticing our breath as we breathe in and out can remind us of the impermanence of life and the inevitability of death, and sitting in loving awareness transforms our hearts so that we live and die in love. Dying into loving awareness, over and over again, being here now, learning to let go of attachments, becoming wiser and more compassionate. And of course, you know from your experience that sitting with the dying is not just good service but great sadhana. Being with people who are dying is living on the edge of awakening. It brings me close to Maharaj-ji, close to the mystery, and opens my heart to love."

Frank, who has worked with the dying for many years at San Francisco's Zen Hospice Project and who trains caregivers with Ram Dass and others through the Metta Institute, asks Ram Dass about his advice for being with the dying.

"You have to be a loving rock," Ram Dass says, "so the dying person can push against you and feel confident. That steadiness comes from your sadhana. If you identify with your soul, you don't get frightened. My favorite practice for being with the dying is loving awareness. Appreciating that we're here, that we're two human beings on the edge of the mystery, we can share our truth together. We are meeting as two souls. This is the moment of living truth. We can't hide. Loving awareness is our spiritual self. It starts from your heart, not your mind. Feel your heart space, feel loving awareness, and repeat silently, 'I am loving awareness.'"

Ram Dass goes on to say that in order to stay in that space of loving, nonjudgmental awareness—not trying to fix anything or to lead the person in a particular direction—we need to prepare ourselves by becoming as free as possible from our own fears of death, from attachment to the dying person, and from wishing things were other than they are. Then we are more likely to be able to be still, relaxed, simple, genuine, and present.

The dying person may be in pain or in a state of agitation or sadness, which is hard to watch, but unless you are responsible for the appropriate medical interventions, it is your simple, nonjudgmental presence and small loving gestures that will be most supportive. When your mind is quiet and your heart is open, there is room for all that is actually happening and whatever else is possible.

Frank asks, "How can technology help us bring love to the dying?"

"I am grateful that technology has allowed me to have a global sangha," Ram Dass responds. "I meet with people from all around the world, and we have what we call heart-to-heart conversations. One day on Skype, I met with a guy in a cave in Russia. The other day, I talked to someone who is struggling with love. He is afraid of deep love, afraid of getting lost in it. I told him that I am a bhakti yogi, the path of ultimate union through love, and that on that path, one intentionally gets lost in love. Then I told him that I loved him, and he haltingly said that he loved me too. That helped him. I had reflected his soul."

Frank adds, "And there is CaringBridge, which helps you build a website for the dying person so that friends and loved ones can stay updated. That helps the dying person feel more relaxed."

Listening to Frank and Ram Dass, I think that being with the dying is powerful training in compassion. The awareness of the universality of death and loss can be a source of connection and solidarity with others in our lives. Then, when we hear about the suffering and death of others, or about those living in fear of suffering and death, we feel connected; we want to relieve that suffering.

BEING WITH THE DYING

No coming, no going.
No after, no before.
I hold you close.
I release you to be free.
Because I am in you,
And you are in me.

THICH NHAT HANH

DRAWN TO THE DYING

his afternoon we decide to talk about how to be with the dying. I've been with only a few dying people—my mother, my sister, my friend Mary McClelland, whom I mentioned earlier—but Ram Dass has been with many. He has often said it is the best way to learn about death.

"That experience of being so close to another human being must change your relationship to others as well," I say.

"That's true," he says. "It changed me." Then he adds, "You know, I've gone through stages in dealing with death. When I was a psychologist, I was interested in the psychological responses to death from an academic distance—denial, anger, fear, bargaining, depression, loss, grief, acceptance, and so on. And then I met Elisabeth Kübler-Ross and Stephen Levine.

"Elisabeth sparked my interest in working with people who were dying. She was intensely fond of that work and made it very exciting. She was interested in the psychological and astral dimensions. Elisabeth has exquisitely described the stages people go through as they approach death—the resistance, the denial, the bargaining, the anger, the despair, and then the opening space. The beauty of her book *On Death and Dying* is that it includes hard data designed to convince the scientific community.

"In 1976, at Boston University, I said to her, 'You have a hard row to hoe to convince the scientific community. I decided a long time ago to just become it. Don't prove anything to anybody.' She said, 'Well, you and I have different dharmas.' Elisabeth did it with no attachment, no clinging, very lightly. I said to her, 'Isn't it remarkable how many thousands of beings I've met and lectured to this year? So many beings are sitting here with us,

Elisabeth, interested in this, sharing this kind of consciousness.' She said, 'Well, don't you remember? We're *all* on death row.'"

"What else do you remember about Elisabeth?" I ask Ram Dass.

"I remember she once came to a retreat I gave, and she was caught smoking."

"I guess she had reached the acceptance stage on smoking," I say.

Ram Dass laughs. Then he is quiet again, thinking, before he says, "Later Stephen [Levine] introduced me to the spiritual dimension of death." A long pause. "The AIDS epidemic hit. Why did I get so deeply involved? I've only recently understood that it was my homosexuality that drove me to be at the bedside of these guys who were dying. I sat with AIDS patients in San Francisco, Boston, and New York."

"I remember at the time you said you realized it could easily have been you. Was that why?" I ask.

"I was so frightened of getting AIDS that I kept away from other gay men. But then I was asked to sit at their bedsides. These men were getting AIDS from sex, and they were afraid of dying. I was afraid of getting AIDS but not afraid of dying. Oh boy, this is hard to see . . . and hard to admit. I was so attracted to them, to the intimacy of bedside relationship. Oh boy! Oy!"

I am smiling. I get it. "You could say that was Maharaj-ji's way of drawing you in to something you needed to learn deeply. Did Maharaj-ji ever ask you about being gay?"

"Gay? He never even mentioned my being Jewish!" Ram Dass is laughing.

TOGETHER AS SOULS

Ram Dass has said that it is hard for us to be with a dying person until we learn how to see what is eternal, so we can be there together as souls. It's simple, but it's not easy. A dying person needs you to be fully there, just being, listening for what is needed with love and kindness but not trying to impose ideas of how to die. Just being what he calls "a loving rock," appreciating that you're here, that you're two human beings on the edge of the mystery, and that you can share your truth together. You are not your roles. You are two souls. This is it. This is the moment of living truth. You can't hide. Ram Dass says it's like God is saying, "C'mon, c'mon in."

"When my mother died," he tells me, "we were drawn together in a whole special way that we hadn't been in this lifetime. Drawn together by just the truth between us. But she had to ask me for my truth, and I had to be ready to give it. And you have to be ready too, not with *my* words but with *your* truth."

He is quiet for a while. And then a flood of words comes, as if he had never had the stroke. This happens rarely, and it is stunning when it does.

"The wisest beings with whom I have made contact in this lifetime all assure me that a soul leaves the physical plane neither a moment too early nor a moment too late. For most of us on earth who so strongly identify with our own bodies and personalities, this is hard to accept. If we have not listened deeply enough inside ourselves to know differently, we consider length of life an asset, which makes it difficult to be with the dying without trying to keep them alive.

"However, once one begins to look at life from the soul's point of view, the picture is quite different. The spirit of Emmanuel, who is channeled through Pat Rodegast, says a human birth is a bit like enrolling in the fourth grade. We stay just as long as it is necessary to achieve what we need from that specific grade, and then we are ready to go on for further evolution by leaving this plane. From the soul's point of view, death is a gift. It is grace that quickens your spiritual work on earth."

"Yes. It takes a leap of understanding," I say, "a leap of faith—like the leap Hanuman took from India to Sri Lanka to save Sita in the Ramayana. Immense."

"It does, so people need support," Ram Dass continues. "When I started the Dying Project in the seventies with Stephen and Ondrea [Levine] and Dale Borglum, our intention was to create a humane and spiritually supportive environment for this kind of transformative work. I gave hundreds of lectures, led retreats, and formed hospices and training programs for spiritual support of the dying.

"I sat quietly with many people who were dying amid the often panicked, frightened, confused feelings of their families. All I had to do was keep my heart open and not get caught in my reactions to the situation or deny them. I learned to cultivate certain qualities—fearlessness and, most important, love. I learned that when I could bring soul quietness, a feeling that everything that was happening was all right, we could come to share a place of intuitive wisdom behind our egos' fears and resistance. I learned to be a loving rock to push against—listening, giving strength, awake, and receptive.

"An intimate encounter with the mystery of death is so profound that it can challenge our most basic beliefs and cherished views. We see amazing change and growth, even at the end of life. At the Metta Institute, we teach caregivers to honor the mystery. We help them develop the willingness to not know and to find humility among the unanswerable questions."

"It's such good work," I say. "I hope I'll be surrounded with that kind of love and understanding when I die. I know *you* will be." Right now, I am appreciating Ram Dass—his service, his kindness, his love—even more deeply than before. Then I hear the sound of chopping vegetables from the kitchen and laughter. It's reassuring.

And it's time for lunch.

A LOVING ROCK

When we sit down again in his room after lunch, I ask Ram Dass, "What else should we say about being with the dying?"

"Learning to be a loving presence for the dying is a practice. You have to open to a deeper part of yourself. It helps to have training, but even if you don't, you can be a comforting presence, as I was when I first started doing this work."

Then he talks for a long time again, giving more suggestions.

"Be natural and relaxed. Learn to feel comfortable with silence. Sit close to the person. They will feel your presence. Just like in meditation, many thoughts and emotions will come up while you are sitting there. The practice is to notice what you are thinking and feeling and, without judging yourself, to bring your attention back to the person who is dying. The intimacy of the connection becomes a soul-to-soul lifeline. The quiet appreciation of the total situation and its possibilities steadily moves things forward. The challenge is to remain in a space of compassion, reverence for life, and acceptance of death—letting the dying person know that you know they are dying, and resting in loving awareness, in communion with the one who is dying.

"As people move closer to dying, they often cope with questions about meaning and purpose. They may experience doubt, uncertainty, regret, and sadness. We can't answer their questions, but we can listen carefully and give support as they work out answers for themselves. We listen to their beliefs, fears, dreams, and struggles with quiet, loving presence.

"If you are a family member or loved one, it's important to say good-bye and to reassure the dying person that those left behind will miss them but that they will be all right.

'It's okay to let go. You are not alone.' This loving reassurance, which releases the dying person from concern, is a great gift at this time."

I say, "People have told me they sometimes feel helpless when they are sitting with the dying. They think, *Why can't I stop this? Why can't I help? Am I doing the right thing? What do you do when that happens?*"

Ram Dass says, "It's about identifying with being rather than doing. The doctors and nurses are doing. You can just *be*. Just be love—a loving rock, loving awareness."

"The months when my sister Barbara was dying," I tell Ram Dass, "I kept having to let go of who she had been, or who I thought she had been. Because of her dementia, she didn't always know who I was, but she knew I was close to her, and she liked being with me. It was actually a great relief."

Ram Dass says, "It's interesting to notice, as loved ones change, how much we often hold on to who they used to be. As people approach their death, they are changing very rapidly. You can practice imagining that you are meeting a dying friend or loved one for the first time each time you visit them, giving up your expectations and judgments, not focusing on who they used to be but just being there."

"Yes, that's what it was like," I say. "Every day was different, new. Toward the end, she was quiet most of the time, and thoughts about death would arise for me: *Will I die soon? Will I be ready? Will I know Dahlia well enough before I die? What happens after death anyhow?*"

Ram Dass responds, "Being with the dying is a precious opportunity to learn about death, but only if you can let go of fear and anxiety. It's good to notice the sensations in your body as they begin to arise. Notice the fear and the thought attached to it. Pay attention. Let go. Remember that you are a soul. Return to the dying person with loving awareness.

"Cultivate humility and equanimity. Humility in the face of the mystery helps us with the frustration we often feel when we think we are supposed to know it all and be in control of it all, when really we're not. We are merely instruments for a process to go on. You are only one part of the whole unfolding."

I find a poem by the great Tibetan teacher Patrul Rinpoche I have brought with me today. It's a slightly irreverent translation by my friend, the monk Matthieu Ricard. "This could be a sitting-by-the-bed poem," I say and share it with Ram Dass:

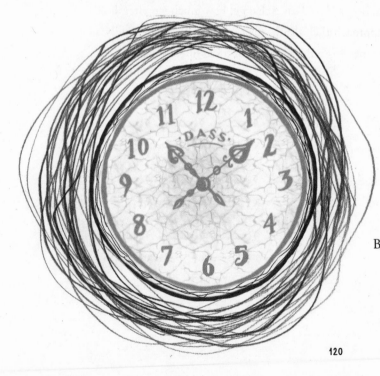

Don't ruminate about the past!
Don't anticipate the future!
Don't cogitate about the present!
Not tampering with it
Leave mind just as is
This very instant
Aware
Relaxed
Beyond this, there's not a damn thing!

"That's good," Ram Dass says. "When you are witnessing the universe unfolding as it should, including you playing your part, you can do it with peace in your heart. Just do what you can without feeling it has to come out a certain way."

"With Barbara I learned a few lessons," I tell Ram Dass. "Smile often. Gentle, light touch communicates love. Holding her hand was simple and comforting. It didn't matter if she remembered my name or that I was her sister. What mattered was that I was there. I did my part, and then what happened, happened. I tried to provide a space of peace for her, and to be there in love, to radiate love.

"And it's important to take care of yourself, especially when the process of dying is long. If you need to go for a walk, do. Don't feel guilty. What's most important is that you are fully there with the dying person. Our friend Sunanda was sitting and meditating with her friend Joyce, who was dying in a Montreal hospital. It had been a long year, and a long day, and it was hard to stay awake. She told me, 'I was sitting next to the bed, being a loving rock, but I was also reading a mystery. I hoped that my loving self was being transmitted. Joyce knew how much I love mysteries, and I didn't fall asleep.'"

Ram Dass says, "You can't take away death, but you can be there in love and comfort as the dying person goes through the changes that lead to death. Sit close enough so that they feel your oneness. You are serving each other by helping each other let go of fear. Alone it is a daunting task; together you enter something bigger than yourself. Love is more powerful than fear."

I tell him, "When my mother was dying of lung cancer in the hospital, she had trouble breathing. In her last couple of days, I would climb into bed with her, which I had not done since I was little. Even when I was little, I don't remember much close bodily affection from my mother. But now, I climbed into bed with her and spooned her, with her back against my front, and I just breathed deeply and slowly. And soon her breathing came into rhythm with mine, and she could relax and breathe."

"That's good," Ram Dass says.

"And when I would get up, her breathing would get irregular again, gaspy. I felt like I was supporting her as she got ready."

"Of course. Intimate. Beautifully intimate," Ram Dass says. "Before Dad died, we had intimacy."

"Holding hands with George?" I ask.

"And meditating together," Ram Dass says, "in a loving place."

We sit for a while, remembering our parents.

Then Ram Dass says, "Suffering is grace; it is part of the process of life itself. Knowing this gives you the ability to stay open to the pain. To the extent that you can rest in that balance and understanding, you can experience the human heart. And even though your heart hurts and keeps breaking, you're still here. And that will help relieve the suffering of your loved one. Do your sadhana now so you can be present enough to accompany the dying person to the last moment of their death."

Many traditions believe that the soul does not leave the body immediately, that it withdraws slowly. Tibetan Buddhists believe it can take from twenty minutes to three weeks. In some traditions, people meditate, pray, chant, or read from sacred texts at this time. In other traditions, it is important to cry and keen and wail, so the departing soul is free to go.

Ram Dass says, "The most important thing is to hold the person in your heart with love."

GUIDELINES FOR BEING A
LOVING ROCK FOR THE DYING

- Be yourself.

- Be compassionately present.

- Be humble.

- Be with each moment.

- Have confidence in the dying process. Trust in the unfolding.

- Don't lose your sense of humor.

- Expect nothing and be ready for anything.

- Let go of your own fears.

- Follow the lead of the dying.

- Practice sacred listening.

- Don't talk about the afterlife unless you are asked.

- Most of all: be love; send love.

LAST LEAF ON THE TREE

onight we are going to a Seva Foundation concert to honor Ram Dass, at the Maui Arts and Cultural Center. I give Ram Dass time to rest and to visit with Joan Baez, who will sing at the concert. After their chat, before leaving for the sound check, Joan says good-bye to us. "It was like a visit with the sun," she tells us. She is beaming. At the concert, she dedicates Tom Waits's song "Last Leaf" to Ram Dass:

> I'm the last leaf on the tree.
> The autumn took the rest, but they won't take me. . . .

> I'll be here through eternity
> If you want to know how long
> If they cut down this tree,
> I'll show up in a song.

It reminds me of ethnobotanist Terence McKenna saying, "I'll try to be around and about. But if I'm not, then you know that I'm behind your eyelids, and I'll meet you there."[11]

GRIEVING

It becomes hard to trust yourself.
All you can depend on now is that
Sorrow will remain faithful to itself.
More than you, it knows its way
And will find the right time
To pull and pull the rope of grief
Until that coiled hill of tears
Has reduced to its last drop.

Gradually, you will learn acquaintance
With the invisible form of your departed;
And when the work of grief is done,
The wound of loss will heal
And you will have learned
To wean your eyes
From that gap in the air
And be able to enter the hearth
In your soul where your loved one
Has awaited your return
All the time.

JOHN O'DONOHUE, "FOR GRIEF"

THE PROFOUND SADNESS OF LOSS

*T*he sky is gray today, and I can't see the horizon, just whitecaps on the water. Before I meet with Ram Dass, I decide to take a few hours to read about grief. Ram Dass's bookshelves hold many books about it—individual grief, family grief, even societal grief. I sit in the living room reading, sipping miso soup, and looking at a sculpture of the monkey god Hanuman, the embodiment of loving service. In the next room, Lucian is watching the news. Trump is saying that the press is the enemy of the American people. I think that much of American society is in grief over the apparent loss of compassion, care, wisdom, and even humor in our leadership.

Grief is the internal part of loss, our emotional response when someone we are deeply connected to leaves or dies or when a dream in life or anything we've invested in is lost.

We may feel lost, alone, sad, empty, abandoned, out of touch with our hearts, without a way to comfort ourselves. Grief can manifest physically as aches and pains or cognitively as an inability to concentrate. It can close our hearts to others, challenging our relationships. Grief affects everyone: the dying person, the caregiver, family, friends, and lovers. It can arise before death, a response in anticipation of the loss to come or to all the losses in the course of an illness—loss of health, social roles, the abilities to speak or move around. Grief is not an event but a process. It is as individual as each of us and as unique as the person we've lost. And it usually means that we feel separate, disconnected.

Every tradition has stories of mourning and grieving. After Lazarus died, Jesus went to the village of Bethany, where Lazarus was buried. When Jesus saw Martha and the other mourners weeping, he also wept. He was moved by their grief and also by the fact of Lazarus's death. Even though Jesus knew he would raise Lazarus from the dead, he chose to mourn with the others. Or maybe it was their sincere grief that led him to revive Lazarus.

Just before going upstairs, I look at some Buddhist texts on grief. Life is impermanent. Don't cling. Give up attachment to the one you have lost. Practice self-compassion. Thich Nhat Hanh wrote, "My pain is like a river of tears, so full it fills up all the four oceans."

Then I read the story of a grieving woman who goes to the Buddha with her dead baby and asks him for medicine to bring the baby back to life. "If you want to make some medicine, you must have some mustard seeds," the Buddha tells her. "Go into town and ask at each house, but you must only accept seeds from a house in which no one has died."

The woman cannot find a seed because she hears of a death at every home: "My father died." "My mother died." "My child died." In the evening, she returns to the Buddha and is no longer carrying the little bundle. Her face is now much calmer. "Have you been able to find the mustard seeds?" he asks. "No," she replies, "but now I understand that everyone loses people they love. I am like everyone else. That has helped me to let go of my grief. I have laid my baby to rest, and I am now at peace. Thank you."

"You have done well," the Buddha tells her, "for there is nothing stronger in all the world than a mother's love. Would you like to stay with me for a while?" As the sun goes down, she and the Buddha talk. She tells him about her life and the baby she loved so dearly. He listens with kindness and reminds her that plants grow in the spring, flower in the summer, and die in the winter—and that new plants grow the following year.

People have their own natural unfolding. They are born and eventually die. She now understands that is how things are.

I climb the stairs, reminded once again that death is inevitable, grief is natural, and we can learn from it and grow. The kindness of friends and teachers helps. I open the door, and there is Ram Dass, kind friend and teacher. He is sitting and watching the ocean. As I join him, I feel the rhythm of my heart blending with the waves of the ocean. I know we should start our conversation, but I am completely content simply to breathe. Ram Dass is quiet too.

"What shall we talk about today?" he asks after a while.

"How about grief?" I say. "I think it's important. People sometimes feel guilty about grieving, like they are not 'spiritual' enough. They feel like they are a drain on their friends. It compounds their guilt. What should we say?"

Ram Dass closes his eyes for a while. Then he says, "Grief is part of the fabric of a human incarnation. To be in a human body means that you will have all of the feelings that that generates: pity, sadness, empathy, horror, beauty, joy, grief, all of it. Our humanity is as much our truth as our divinity is. To deny either one of them is to go astray. The humanity wants to take away the suffering; the divinity delights in the unfolding. Grief helps us accept the profound sadness of loss and then folds it into the wholeness of life. You don't heal from grief. You reconnect with your loving soul, which was never grieving, never traumatized, always free."

I say, "I think that going through suffering makes us more real, more human. I realized at one point that I am drawn to people who have suffered because they are wiser, more present. We don't wish suffering on ourselves or anyone, but it is the way we grow."

"When I sit with the family of the dead," Ram Dass shares, "I usually take the high road, the soul road. When I worked with Frank Ostaseski, who is a master of the psychological level, he would talk to people about what they are feeling, taking them through the mud. Both are important at those times."

THE HEALING POWER OF LOVE

Girija Brilliant, cofounder of Seva Foundation, recently told me that her favorite times with her late son Jon, who died when he was twenty-six, were becoming harder to remember, and that felt like another level of losing him.

Ram Dass says, "The soul never dies, and loved ones who die are still present in a different form. Death ends a life, but not the relationship. But most of us still need to grieve, especially if the dead person was young or the death was sudden, and sometimes just to feel close to the one who is gone."

He continues, "It's hard when it is someone you love deeply, but death is the end of a body, not a soul. It isn't the end of your relationship with your loved one; it is an invitation to form a new relationship, soul to soul. When you are quiet enough, you realize that love is never lost, that they haven't gone anywhere. The love that you share is invulnerable to the winds of time. In fact, everybody you have ever loved is part of the fabric of your being now."

I say, "Do you remember the story of Maharaj-ji suddenly looking up and saying that an old woman, a great devotee, had just died? Then he laughed. A devotee who was with him asked why he wasn't grieving, and Maharaj-ji answered, 'What do you want me to do, act like one of the puppets? The body dies, but not the soul.'"

Ram Dass says slowly, "One of the puppets . . ."

Then I say, "My friend Barry Boyce's nephew died, and he was asked to do the service. His nephew had had a troubled life, so Barry asked Frank [Ostaseski] what to say. Frank encouraged him to ask the family to acknowledge and hold everything about this boy, not just the things they approved of, but everything about him, so that their grieving could be honest and full.

"Frank said, 'Each of us has our light, what makes us loving and lovable. Each of us has our dark places, how we grapple with fear and pain—which can make us unbearable at times, even to ourselves. We have our glory and our griminess. So when you think of the loved one who has passed, embrace the whole person.'"

Ram Dass looks mischievous. He responds, "Well, last week, I offered to say a few words for the burial of Luv, our cat. I said that he was named after Ram's son and that he gave solace to others by cuddling up. He was born in the basement of a restaurant in Makawao, and he looked for a good home. That good home was our hearts. I didn't say anything about the naughty things [he did] or that he slept most days in a closet or that he was fat."

"I think you are forgiven!" I say.

We laugh, and then Ram Dass moves to another subject without missing a beat. Being with him, I realize again and again that there is no separation between life, death, cats, grieving parents—they are part of a seamless whole. We don't need to say, "And now, on a more serious note . . . "

But Ram Dass does go on in a serious tone. "Some years ago, a couple lost their child and asked me for guidance. I wrote a letter. Many people have read it."

Dear Steve and Anita,

Rachel finished her work on earth and left the stage in a manner that leaves those of us left behind with a cry of agony in our hearts, as the fragile thread of our faith is dealt with so violently. Is anyone strong enough to stay conscious through such a teaching as you are receiving? Probably very few. And even they would only have a whisper of equanimity and peace amidst the screaming trumpets of their rage, grief, horror, and desolation.

I can't assuage your pain with any words, nor should I. For your pain is Rachel's legacy to you. Not that she or I would inflict such pain by choice, but there it is. And it must burn its purifying way to completion. For something in you dies when you bear the unbearable, and it is only in that dark night of the soul that you are prepared to see as God sees and to love as God loves.

Now is the time to let your grief find expression. No false strength. Now is the time to sit quietly and speak to Rachel, to thank her for being with you these few years and encourage her to go on with whatever her work is, knowing that you will grow in compassion and wisdom from this experience. In my heart, I know that you and she will meet again and again and recognize the many ways in which you have known each other. And when you meet, you will know, in a flash, what now it is not given you to know: why this had to be the way it was.

Our rational minds can never understand what has happened, but our hearts—if we can keep them open to God—will find their own intuitive way. Rachel came through you to do her work on earth, which includes her manner of death. Now her soul is free, and the love that you can share with her is invulnerable to the winds of changing time and space.

In that deep love, include me.

In love,
Ram Dass

"Some time after that, I received a letter from a man who worked on the Ford assembly line in Detroit. He said that his son, twenty-three years old, had gone to Hawaii on a vacation with some friends. They went snorkeling; it was the first time for all of them. His son was a healthy athlete and a good swimmer. After they'd been there for a while, his friends saw that he was staying down a long time. When they brought him up, he was brain-dead. They put him on a respirator. The father flew to Hawaii and at great expense flew his son back in an ambulance plane to the mainland. After a few weeks, the dad had to be responsible for pulling the plug on the respirator to watch his son die.

"He talked about what a wonderful boy his son was, what a wonderful job he had. He was a devoted son, who would never stay out late at night without calling home so that his parents wouldn't worry. 'They say that God is perfect,' this father told me, 'but all I can think of is that God made a mistake. I cannot believe there would be any good reason to allow this to happen. Three lives have been destroyed, not just one. My wife is a truly great woman, and she did not deserve this. I'm sixty years old, and she's fifty. He was our future. Now everything seems futile and empty, and I wake up crying every morning. I feel it's cruel to send my son off into eternal life because he doesn't know anyone there. Only his grandparents on my wife's side are there before him, but he never knew them because they passed away when he was very young. To think of him as lonely makes it unbearable for me. People keep explaining it as an accident. I don't believe this was an accident. I can reiterate eight or nine things that happened as I look back over the months that preceded this tragedy, and we see that it was all leading up to the occurrence. I won't go into them now, but I think something was there.'"

"Raghu sent me the letter you wrote back to him," I say. "I'll read it to you."

I feel such pain for the loss that you and your wife have suffered. The grief that parents experience at the loss of a child is perhaps the deepest grief of all because it seems to upset the natural order of things. What I can share with you from a spiritual vantage point cannot really allay your grief. Perhaps, however, it will allow you and your son to know each other in another way, and that other way of knowing may give balance to the grief.

Because your son was attractive and was your son, so warm and vibrant, you got to know him through his uniqueness and his separateness. There is another way of knowing a person, which we know through our intuitive heart. This way of knowing one another is subtle, and so it is often hidden behind the more obvious ways of knowing people through the senses and thought. But if we know what to look for and cultivate that intuitive way of knowing, we find out for ourselves that we are each indeed more than just body and personality. While no name is entirely satisfactory for this other dimension of ourselves, for the purpose of our discussion, the word "soul" will do.

And what is this soul? It is a unique entity, which clothes itself in a personality and body when the time is right to take birth on the physical human plane. This personality and body are much like spacesuits for dwelling on earth. Inevitably, in all but the rarest cases, within a few years, the infant becomes so strongly identified with its spacesuit that it loses its memory of its original identity as a soul. Then we live out life engaged in our human vocations until our death, when we leave behind the spacesuit and once again remember our true selves as souls.

Now the soul itself has an agenda in taking birth as a human being. It has certain work to do and complete while on the earth plane. It uses the body and personality to carry out this work, and when this work is finished, it leaves this plane.

The wisest beings with whom I have made contact in this lifetime all assure me that a soul leaves the physical plane neither a moment too early nor a moment too late.

Now to us on Earth, who so strongly identify with our bodies and personalities, this is hard to understand. Because we have usually not listened deeply enough inside ourselves to know different, we consider duration in life an asset. We tend to think of the earth plane as the be-all and end-all, so that we want to make it last as long as possible. However, once one begins to look at life from the soul's point of view, the picture is quite different. A human birth is a bit like enrolling in the fourth grade, and we stay as long as necessary to achieve what we need from that specific grade, or form, and then we are naturally ready to go on for further evolution by leaving this plane.

I can sense, from your description of your son and from the pictures, the purity of his heart and the beauty of his soul. I suspect that though you considered his work on earth was just beginning, for his soul the work was completed. Even the manner of his leaving was part of his work. Now, I realize that for you it is inconceivable that a son who would call when he was going to be late at night could possibly leave you in such a fashion by choice. But you see, it was not his personality's choice; it was his soul's choice. His personality, in fact, would never be able to leave you because of the power of the bond of human-attached love that existed between you and your wife and him.

But the soul is not limited by human-attached love because it knows and is joined to others by what is sometimes called the "love that surpasseth understanding." It is conscious, or spiritual, love. It is the love that Christ shared with his father. It is the same love that binds you and Keith together far more deeply than even the human love of father and son. Now, when your grief is at its strongest, it is hard to tune in to this deeper love, especially since it makes no rational sense. However, you already have intimations, and later it will become much clearer to you that the true love you and your son share is untouched by these recent events.

In the dimension where this love exists, this soul love, there is neither coming nor going. That love is not vulnerable to time or changes in form. Only when your mind will be quiet enough will your heart give you the reassurance that you seek, that the essence of the love is still very much with you. This in no way will negate the pain of the loss of his form, to which you were deeply attached, but it will balance that loss with a new opportunity. Now that his captivating form is no longer present, you are freer to make contact with his soul, especially as you are able to acknowledge your own.

The question of whether your life has been destroyed by this event is another point that is touched by our discussion. For your personality, the pain is shattering and seemingly unbearable. I have no doubt that you awaken crying and now find life meaningless. Suffering is what the personality would avoid at all costs if it were able. For your soul, however, it is an entirely different matter. For your soul, suffering is that which forces you to grow spiritually and brings you closer to awakening to who you in truth are.

I realize, even as I say all these things to you, that it is really too much for me to ask of you that you understand the way in which the manner of your son's death was his soul's gift to your soul. I suspect all that seems topsy-turvy to you. But you did ask me how I understood such tragic events, and this is my truth, which I'm honored to share with you. However, from the tone of your letter, the premonitions, et cetera, I suspect that you are riper to hear these things than even you suspect.

Now, as to how your son is, I can only intuit that a moment after he left his body, after leaving a thread of consciousness in his body for some weeks to give you a chance to adjust to the loss and to give you the opportunity to help him along the way, he was filled with an indescribable light of the most profound love. Even though there were not people familiar to him from his stay on Earth to greet him, there were many beings most familiar to his soul ready to welcome him.

But probably your suffering and your attachment to him and sense of loss are felt by his soul. Although he understands what has happened, why it had to happen the way it did, and why you are suffering as you are, I'm sure he's surrounding you with healing energy. And as you're able to quiet your mind, I suspect that you will feel it—it of course acts to your benefit even if you don't feel it. To the extent that you're able to sit quietly and just hang out with your son, talk to him as you normally would about the many experiences you shared together. But in doing so, look to see the thread of spirit that pervaded each experience. Imagine that you and he are souls who met on Earth this time as father and son. How many times in your years together did the love between you nearly rend the veil of mystery that would have allowed you to recognize the truth of soul that lay at the root of your relationship?

It takes only a moment for two people to recognize their bond as souls, for souls know no time. And now, even though your son is no longer embodied, you and he can recognize each other. In no way do I think there was an error on your part in removing the life-support system. Your hand was guided by deeper forces of truth within yourself. Under such conditions we do what must be done. Let your mind be at ease about this. Were it not your son's time to leave his body, there is no way you could have done what you did; you were just playing your part.

I suspect that when the loss of the form burns its way through and you deal with the desolation and the grief and the sense of separateness, and can quiet down just a bit and sit with it, you will start to feel in your heart, if you can listen very carefully, a very deep and profound loving connection that is not just a memory but a living truth—and that will start to nurture you.

My guru, who is the closest being I have ever had in my life, closer than my parents or any lover, left his body in 1973. Now, all these years later, he is the closest being in my life. And he is a living truth that I live with every day. The fact that he isn't in his form makes me understand him in much more profound ways than I ever would have had he remained in form. I could keep his form at a distance. The love that we finally meet in is something that is inside each other. When you love somebody enough to miss them, you've touched them in true conscious love. We get so attached to our senses and thoughts about a person as object that we feel desperate when we lose them; we feel we've lost something. Then we quiet down, and we realize that we've moved to a new level of richness of being together.

In love,
Ram Dass

FROM MOURNING TO REMEMBERING

We sit in silence for a while. We both know that the loss of a child is probably the worst suffering one can experience in this life. Several of our close friends have lost their children. I try to imagine it, but when my son, Owen, comes into my mind, it closes down before I can even imagine him dead.

At this moment, I remember being in India at Maharaj-ji's temple in the eighties, when my mother was taken to the hospital. I had been there only a short time, but I had to go home to be with her. I went to Siddhi Ma to say good-bye. I had been so happy there, sitting next to Maharaj-ji's bed with his picture and plaid blanket, drinking chai, walking the paths at "cow dust" time, watching the sun set behind the temples, chanting along with the *kirtan* wallahs, my heart so open, love so present—but when I said good-bye, I began to cry. I cried as I bowed to Siddhi Ma, I cried as I gathered my things and put them in the car, and I cried as I said good-bye to the staff. I cried in the car for hours with Ramesh, all the way to Delhi. I cried in grief for my mother, and for leaving India, and for Maharaj-ji, and for all the brokenness in my heart. During that stream of tears, I realized that when you open your heart to any one emotion, including happiness, it is open to all emotions, including sadness and regret and heartbreak and grief. As Maharaj-ji said often, *Sub ek*—"All one."

Ram Dass offers, "Grief is one of our greatest teachers. It cracks us open—that's how the light gets in. It demands that we look at our relationship with life and our fear of death. It reveals the great healing power of love.

"My way of supporting grieving is to say: Grieve. My God, grieve. Don't try to stop grieving. Don't pretend to have strength when you don't because it looks good—go grieve some more. Grieve in a way that is true to your being. It's just as untrue to grieve when you're not feeling it as not to grieve when you're feeling it. Just allow the human pain. Don't hide it; just keep going through it. Grieving is not a sign of weakness but of strength. It takes courage to go through it.

"At the same time, take care of yourself. Grief comes in waves. It can seem to be over and then come back and overwhelm you. You may feel like you are the one who is dying, and some part of you may be, or you may experience guilt, anger, or loneliness.

"This is the time to remember that everything, even grief, is impermanent. It will transform into something else. Change may come in an *aha!* moment, or it may be a series of small insights. But it will come.

"If you don't grieve fully, in a way that is true to your own heart, you may end up with cynicism about life and fear of future involvement, fear of any risk. Be kind to yourself. When it is time to let go, you'll know. Then let go. The memories will still be there, without the attachment. It's not about returning to 'normal,' but becoming someone new, free to be present for whatever your life is now."

I ask him, "Do you remember [Rabbi] Alan Lew? He was a friend. We taught together. Norman Fischer taught with him also, and they brought together the teachings of Buddhist and Jewish spirituality. After Alan died suddenly, Norman wrote: 'Loss wounds the heart, causing it to fall open. Love rushes into and out of the opening. Love that was probably there all along, but you didn't notice because you were busy with so many things that you couldn't feel it. Love rushes in to the absence left by loss. And that love brings inspired action. If we are able to give ourselves to the loss, to move toward it instead of away, our wounded hearts become full.'"

Ram Dass says, "Loss . . . move toward it instead of away from it. Yeah. Norman loved the rabbi."

"He did. Very much. And they shared their faith. How would you say faith is related to grieving?"

Ram Dass answers, "In grief, when everything seems dark and chaotic, and we are crying with agony in our hearts, anything that the mind is holding on to as a belief will be very shaky. Belief is rooted in the mind, and in the face of death, the mind crumbles. We doubt everything that we have known to be true. Faith is rooted in the heart. It exists beyond the thinking mind. That's why faith is important, even when it is only a fragile thread.

"Faith is persisting in the presence of doubt so that you can connect to the universal. As your faith in the rhythms of the universe gets deeper, you'll find bedrock, even when things are really shaky. Without faith, you fear. If you have faith, you have no fear.

"One suggestion for times of flickering faith—and grief can be full of those times—is to connect yourself with nature, with rivers and trees and rocks and sky. Feel the impersonality of it all. It only looks bleak from where you are standing. Go out into nature and just lie down on the ground or sit by a river. The running water keeps washing the mind as you watch the leaves float down the river. After some time, the mind becomes less confused and cloudy, so that you are better able to see things as they are."

Looking out at the hibiscus, the coconuts ripening at the tops of palm trees, the bright red ti leaves, agave, papaya, norfolk pines—*they could heal grief*, I think. "I knew someone who went on a pilgrimage," I recall, "walking two hundred miles to Santiago de Compostela in Spain, and somewhere along the route, she cried and cried and then felt her grief lift."

Ram Dass says, "Some people do special practices like that, and some just go through life, hoping and waiting for the grief to change."

"John Perry Barlow said that when he was grieving, he felt like he was a bottomless well of grief, and you said to him, 'Maybe it's not bottomless, just very deep. One day it will fill with love.' That really helped him."

Ram Dass responds, "Well, at some point—and it's different for everybody—we quiet down naturally. We glimpse for the first time a tiny light in the darkness, a first feeling of connection with somebody or something, the possibility of healing into connection again. We begin to move from mourning to remembering."

From mourning to remembering. I walk downstairs remembering that Anne Lamott said losing a loved one is like having a broken leg that never heals perfectly, that still hurts when the weather gets cold, but you learn to dance with the limp.

In the kitchen, I talk with Dassi and Lakshman, enjoying their liveliness, happy I am not grieving their loss. What do we have to eat? Some apple cake left over from last night. It tastes alive, delicious. I am grateful to be here now.

THEY ARE PART OF ME

Later that day I climb the stairs to Ram Dass's room again. He looks quite happy. We reflect on our earlier conversation.

Ram Dass says, "When people we love die, they become part of us."

"But as you just said, people need to go through grief to get to another place."

"I said it, and Norman said it—but all my friends who've died are still here, still with me. I didn't lose anyone. Maharaj-ji is here. And Stephen [Levine]—he populates my mind."

"Is it different from when Stephen was living in New Mexico?" I ask.

"Well, we'd call each other on the phone then. I would bring his comments into myself. Now I bring all of him into myself. Love is reaching out to bring him and others in. Like when I work with Ramesh [Rameshwar Das, coauthor of *Polishing the Mirror*] on my memoir, I have a hard time with the idea that my brothers and father and mother are not living. They *are* around. It's love, just love. I love every one of these people. I've taken them into myself."

"They have become you," I say.

"Yup, yup."

"After my mother died," I tell Ram Dass, "I noticed that I spontaneously moved my hands like she did, and there were inflections in my voice that were hers."

"Wow!"

"And I remember being at the burning ghats in India and breathing in the smoke coming from a burning body, realizing that we *physically* become part of each other. It was only physical, but I understood something. Like you said, you took in Stephen's words—actually took them in. I was taking in the person who was being burned."

Ram Dass says, "That smoke . . . that's great . . . that's transition. I'm sure I did the same thing there. The smell of that smoke, the smell of the person . . . smoke is one level, and love is another level. Love is an incorporation."

"*Incorporation* means 'in your body.' In the corpus."

"Hmm . . . God, this stuff is so tasty," Ram Dass says.

Lakshman arrives. "Are we going to have a little something to eat?" he asks. "You have to be at your doctor's place soon."

"Okay."

Lakshman puts a plate of vegetables and rice and a tortilla on Ram Dass's little side table. He eats for a while and then says, "You know, at first I thought we were writing a book, and I thought it would be work. And then we said 'conversations,' and I thought, *I'm off the hook; this will be fun.*"

"And now?" I ask.

"I trust your consciousness. We are writing the right book—considering my stroke and that I can't write or communicate very well."

"I wouldn't say that you can't communicate well," I tell Ram Dass. "It's a different form of communication. It's pretty great that after all you've said and written over the years that you can still surprise people—like me—with what you say. It's such a confirmation that when we are in the moment, not caught in memory or expectation, there are always new ways of seeing, always something new to learn."

"It's being in the moment. The moment is so choice. Maybe we should call the book *In the Moment*," Ram Dass suggests.

"Pretty much like *Be Here Now*," I say.

"Yeah, I guess so."

BLESSINGS FOR THE JOURNEY

F uneral services and memorials help the friends and family of the dead to process their grief and let go so that the soul can be free. They also celebrate life in all its diversity and strengthen the community. These ceremonies are as unique as the person being remembered and the culture they belong to. I've been to Irish American gatherings, where food and drink are plentiful, and people tell stories and reflect on how the deceased is happy now with their parents and grandparents in heaven. New Orleans has the tradition of jazz funerals, in which a brass band and mourners march toward the ceremony to dirges like "Just a Closer Walk with Thee," and then return from the ceremony celebrating life with upbeat spirituals like "When the Saints Go Marching In." Friends who are not part of the band dance and sing in the second line, behind the musicians. In Hawaii, ashes are taken out to sea in an outrigger canoe and spread in the ocean; back at shore, there are flowers and chanting, and friends "talk story." When a young African American Muslim friend was shot, we gathered together, cried and hugged, and read from the Koran in between sharing stories of his life.

I remember the service for our young friend Anna Mirabai Lytton, who at fourteen years old was hit by a car while riding her bike. We were sitting in the Guild Hall in East Hampton, Long Island, which on most days is a place for films, lectures, and readings by artists and writers with ties to the community. That day, it was a space to remember Anna Mirabai, a sacred space holding sadness, anguish, questions, wisdom, and a strange kind of joy, too, that floated through from the door to the other world. We signed the guest book as we walked in and received a program with a photo of Anna Mirabai smiling in what can only be called a knowing way—like a knowing that everything is happening exactly as it should.

The printed program included a poem by her that ends, "We have reached our resting place and completed our work," which is what Ram Dass says about her passing: "She has completed her work in this life."

Inside the hall, full-screen photos of Anna Mirabai were being projected, one fading into another, loving portraits by her father, Rameshwar Das, and at the same time we listened to music from the playlist found on Anna Mirabai's computer. I saw photos of her playing in the snow, smiling in India, smiling with her brother, James, and her mother, Kate, and I heard "Yesterday" by the Beatles, deeply familiar but with a fresh meaning: these troubles truly did seem so far away yesterday. Old friends were there, as well as Anna Mirabai's school friends, neighbors, and others. Krishna Das took his place behind his harmonium to begin the chanting for the service, telling me later that he was nervous not only because of his grief but also because he saw policemen in uniform and others he thought wouldn't be comfortable with the Hindu chanting: *Sri Ram Jai Ram Jai Jai Ram.* He kept the kirtan short.

I sat between friends, feeling helpless and overwhelmed, sadness rising like the waves on the East Hampton beach. Ramesh walked onto the stage and began to speak: "I hope I can do this," he said. I didn't know how he would, but he continued, "I have been held in the love and prayers of our extended community. You have lifted us and sustained us. We are here to celebrate our beautiful daughter. We are so deeply grateful to so many—to the police who arrived at the scene, to the good Samaritans who lifted the car off her body, to the EMTs and hospital staff who tried to save her. They all treated her as if she were their own child."

I was crying, and Ramesh was barely keeping it together. But his presence was reassuring. He was doing this for all of us.

"I feel blessed to be her parent. Let's have a moment of silence to remember her," he continued. And then, in a very quiet voice, "Imagine love, love washing over you like the waves on the shore . . ."

YOUR OWN DEATH

THE LAST SADHANA

On the day I die,
when I am being carried toward the grave,
don't weep.

Don't say, He's gone. He's gone,
Death has nothing to do with going away.

The sun sets and the moon sets,
but they are not gone.

Death is a coming together.
The tomb looks like a prison,
but it's really release into union.

The human seed goes down in the ground
like a bucket into the well where Joseph is.

It grows and comes up full
of some unimagined beauty.
Your mouth closes here
and immediately opens
with a shout of joy there.

RUMI

A LONG WAY GONE

Before I go to see Ram Dass, I sit on the floor in my room and think about Maharaj-ji. I think of how being loved by him feels like being loved from the inside out. Then I remember that the Tibetans say we leave this life as easily as a hair is pulled from butter. The Upanishads talk about death as a ripe mango or a fig loosened from its branch, falling naturally and easily. But it's not always that way. How can we help others prepare?

When I arrive in Ram Dass's room, I am ready to talk about preparing to die and how that is a spiritual practice. Dassi is there, and Ram Dass is listening to Jackson Brown singing "The Long Way Around": "We're a long way gone, down this wild road we're on . . ." Jackson had sung this for Ram Dass at the Seva concert the other night. Ram Dass says, "That's us: a long way gone." I smile and nod my head.

I ask him, "What shall we tell people about planning for their own death? Siri says 151,600 people die each day."

Ram Dass responds, "Well, each person should die in the way that feels right to them."

"That's important. But if I asked for your advice on how to die, what would you say?"

"First, complete your business in this world—your financial, legal, and family business. Then you won't be distracted by those thoughts. You'll be content that others are taken care of."

I agree and build on that. "I like the idea of spiritual legacy. Telling others your spiritual story before you go, so they can learn from it. That's what you have done. But everyone has a story. I'll put some links in the book's resources section."

"Yes, that's good," Ram Dass says.

Then I say, "Some people avoid making a will. There is a superstition that as long as your will isn't complete, you can't die. But you did write your will recently. Did it bring anything up for you?"

"It brought up stuff—like my son, Peter, and how I wasn't a father all those years for my son," Ram Dass tells me. "I couldn't be because I didn't know about him until he was fifty. And the other Peter [Heil], who was my partner—we are so connected as souls that he calls me and I call him just to be there, but there is no attachment."

Ram Dass continues, "And let people know how you want to die. Name a health proxy and decide how much medication you want, whether you want to be kept on life support, and whether you will be buried or cremated. On Maui now, there are many alternatives, including simple wood coffins and environmentally conscious cremation."

SACRED SPACE

Next, we talk about creating the space to die. I like converting spaces. Each year, in Western Massachusetts, we transform a hundred-year-old barn into a temple to celebrate the anniversary of Maharaj-ji's death. We clean up after the bats that live there, hang Indian batiks on the walls, and create an altar with Maharaj-ji's picture, candles, incense, and flowers. The "normal" is deconstructed to become a place for transformation.

Any place can become a sacred space to die. When you cross the threshold into sacred space, you leave the old world behind and open to the new. Here, death is a part of life, and everything belongs. It is the place where, as we leave the body, we become fully soul.

"If possible," Ram Dass says, "people need to decide before the advent of a crisis where they want to die."

"Where do you want to die?" I think I know, but maybe I'd better check.

"Right over there. In my bed."

It is already a sacred space, just across from a wall-sized weaving of Maharaj-ji that captures the great tenderness in his eyes.

Most Americans agree that they want to die at home, but many die in hospitals or other health-care facilities. Of course, even a hospital can become a sacred space. What is important is that the dying person is comfortable and as supported as possible in letting go into the process. The place should be free of disturbances that might cause negative emotions like regret or anger or sadness.

So how can we create a spiritual atmosphere in the space where our biological functions will cease, no matter where it is?

Ram Dass and I decide that it is helpful to have fresh air, natural light if possible, flowers, or other natural objects. In some traditions, people create an altar with the four elements: earth, air, fire, and water. Sometimes pictures of loved ones or of happy events in the past help the person feel at home, but it is a tricky balance, figuring out whether that photo of the whole family gathered for Thanksgiving will contribute to a space of love or keep the dying person from saying good-bye. Maybe a painting of an angel or a photo of white clouds in a blue sky or an image of the Divine Mother would be more helpful for letting go into soul. In Japan, they often put a screen portraying the heavenly abode at the foot of the bed.

Ram Dass says, "It's like a railway ticket, so you know where you're going and can dally along the way."

In the Sioux tradition, after the power of puberty ceremonies, the youth go into the forest and sit in meditation until they hear their personal death chant. They then use this chant every time they get frightened or approach a death experience during life, so that when death happens, they know their way through.

Ram Dass adds, "I want a picture of Maharaj-ji. No other pictures."

SACRED SOUND

*a*nd then Ram Dass tells me, "I want to hear kirtan for some time. But please . . ." He waits for the right words. "Don't bring a wild band of live musicians." We both laugh. "Then I want silence as I near death."

When my sister Barbara was restless and edgy in her room in the assisted-living home, her daughter, Lisa, and I would put on a CD of harp music and enter a space of meditation with her, saying that there's nothing to hold on to, nothing to do, nowhere to go, just being here now, breathing, floating like a cloud in a vast sky. Then my sister would sink back deeply into her pillow with a little smile on her face, looking like she felt free.

Quiet, restful, meditative music can help create the right atmosphere, as it did for Barbara. The dying person should decide. The harp is a good choice because it is polyphonic and can deliver warm and low, resonant tones. That must be why angels like the harp. Often people ask for their old favorites—Barbara's was Willie Nelson—but make sure you are using music not to entertain or distract the person, but to ease symptoms like pain or restlessness and to help them in the process of letting go. Old favorites may awaken memories and emotions that make it difficult to let go.

PAIN, MEDICATION, AND CONSCIOUSNESS

"I know you have thought a lot about balancing pain, medication, and consciousness," I say to Ram Dass. "In fact, you've had so much pain that you are an expert. What should we say?"

"I want to be as conscious as possible as I transition from the body to the soul," Ram Dass says, "but I don't want to suffer too much. I think it's good to withstand the pain and suffering until you can't—and I say that having experienced a lot of pain. Strong drugs, like morphine, dull consciousness. Morphine is compassionate, but then you may go into your last ceremony asleep. On the other hand, if you're in huge pain, your consciousness is in the pain, so you're not free to be in loving awareness. Usually, it's not a matter of either/or, but of degrees of medicine."

"Good way to think about it," I say.

Ram Dass adds, "It's just a cautionary guideline to create the best balance you can around consciousness and pain. I have also used nonmedical ways to deal with the pain. Pain captures your awareness, but if you move into pure awareness in the midst of it, even for a moment, your relationship with your pain will change. Awareness of pain isn't painful. The pain is in the thought of the pain. If you pay close attention, you'll see that you have thoughts and feelings about the pain—what's causing it, how long it will last, how terrible it is. If you accept and love those thoughts and emotions, it will reduce the pain."

"I have a hard time with pain," I confess, thinking about a recent gum surgery.

"I have neuropathy in my feet, especially at night," says Ram Dass.

"It's really painful, isn't it?"

"Yup, yup, yup."

"And it's related to diabetes, so many people have it."

"I play with it," Ram Dass says. "If I'm having a dark thought, I become aware of the thought and ask myself what I'm doing. My awareness is in my soul, and I bring that awareness to witness the pain in my toes, over and over again, identifying with the awareness, not the pain. The pain is in my mind.

"I often have pain in more than one place, so I move my awareness from my toes to my bladder, from pain to pain. I begin to say, 'God, I'm a mess.' But all that means is that my body is a mess, and I am doing the work of this incarnation with joy. Oy!"

"It's not so easy, though, to rest in awareness during pain," I point out. "I've learned the most from mindfulness practices, being mindful of parts of the body as a sadhana before the pain arrives."

"Definitely," says Ram Dass. "Start now."

When Ram Dass talked before about loving everything, he included suffering and pain. I ask, "What do you mean when you say, 'I love the pain'?"

"Well, if I stay in the witness, in awareness, which is the soul, and the soul loves everything, then everything belongs. It is all lovable," he tells me.

I wish for him that he is always able to do that.

LAST WISHES

Soon Dassi arrives to go over Ram Dass's wishes for his own death. She reads aloud some prepared statements from his living will, called "Five Wishes." Ram Dass has already chosen a health-care proxy and decided what life-support procedures he wants as he approaches death, so Dassi continues with questions about his spiritual and emotional desires—what he wants his loved ones to know and so forth.

Ram Dass answers each question simply: "I wish to die at home, if that is possible, yes.

"I wish to be cared for with kindness and cheerfulness, definitely not sadness.

"I wish to have pictures of my loved ones near my bed: just Maharaj-ji.

"I wish my family and friends to know that I love them, yes.

"I wish my family and friends to know that I did not fear death itself, yes.

"I wish people to think about me as I was before I became seriously ill. This is just my body.

"I wish for my friends to respect my wishes even if they don't agree with them.

"I wish for my family and friends to look at my dying as a time for personal growth for everyone, including me."

Then Ram Dass says, "I want to have friends with me while I am dying, but at the end, I want to be alone with Maharaj-ji.

"I've talked about the body viewing with Dassi; it will be here at the house. Then Bodhi will come with the new hearse and take me to the cremation ground."

"In Hawaiian traditional burial," I note, "they take your body out to sea and put it in the water."

"Yes, but if I did that," Ram Dass responds, "then people who want to visit the site would have to take boats five miles out to sea."

"There could be a flotilla," I tell him, "and when they get there, they could chant what you say when you reach the buoy when swimming in the ocean: 'Oh buoy, oh buoy, oh boy, oh boy!'"

We both laugh, imagining it.

"On Maui," Ram Dass says, "Bodhi and Leila and I started Doorway into Light, which helps people with living wills, advance health-care directives, home funerals, home burial, direct burial, direct cremation, ocean body burial, and organ donation.

"Bodhi and I wanted to design a cremation box with a window, so people could see the fire, but instead Bodhi talked to the public health official about open-air cremation, which they do in India. They have given us a permit, and we have a place for it. I'll be the first."

I take a very deep breath in. I thought I was comfortable with all the details of Ram Dass's leaving. I remember funeral pyres in Benares, the smoke and the smell of burning flesh. *This is going to take some processing*, I think. I breathe out slowly.

"It will be sadhana for everyone watching," Ram Dass says. "That's for sure. Death and sadhana."

"What about your ashes?" I ask. "There will be a lot of them."

Ram Dass responds in a matter-of-fact tone. "You should fill a small white box—the kind you take home from a Chinese restaurant—to take to Taos. Raghu picked out a plot for me at the Hanuman Temple there, so people can visit and call me to mind. The rest of the ashes should be scattered in the ocean here in Maui. There won't be a physical place in Maui for devotees to contact me, but the real place is in their hearts."

Dassi says, "I need your signature here," as she carefully places the paper at a right angle for Ram Dass. "Here's something to lean on. Sign it 'Richard Alpert'"—Ram Dass's legal name.

GIVING UP ATTACHMENT

his evening, before we begin our discussion on giving up attachment as a preparation for death, I look through my notes on the subject. I find this transcript from a talk Ram Dass gave called "Perspectives on Death":

As I studied Buddhism, I learned that the Theravadin Buddhist monks were usually sent to the cemetery for a night, all night, to sit and meditate on the decaying body of a recently dead monk, on the fly-infested corpse, the skeleton, in order to loosen their attachment to the body and to see its ephemeral or changing nature. The purpose is to let go of the attachment to the concept of life being the body, so that during the dying process, instead of being filled with "I'm dying" or "Don't let me die," the monks would be attentive to the moment as each part of the process unfolds.

A lot of the anxiety and struggle during dying has to do with the concept that the person has about what's happening, not with what's actually happening, not the dying process itself. Many dying people struggle terribly hard because they have a model that this is loss and failure—and that's terribly frightening. And yet, for many other dying people, there is a release, an opening, a letting go, a feeling of rightness, which often leaves the doctor and the nurse feeling privileged to be present, feeling graced to be part of this somewhat mysterious process in which a transformation occurred.

Later, Ram Dass tells me, "I had a dream. I was looking down at my funeral, the celebration of my life and death, and I watched people come by the casket. I could see into each person's heart; I knew what they were seeing and thinking. Some of them were of loving heart, others, phony heart. Some were loving family, others were there because I was famous."

"I'll look around at your funeral if I'm there and try to see who has the loving heart," I say.

Ram Dass laughs. "I feel no attachment to the past. Or to the future. I'm in the moment. I can't picture my death because I'm not dying in this moment. . . . I always loved the Third Chinese Patriarch . . ."

"I remember. You used to recite your version of his 'Verses on the Faith-Mind' at lectures."

Ram Dass recites part of it now, from memory:

The Great Way is not difficult
for those who have no preferences.
When not attached to love or hate,
all is clear and undisguised.
Separate by the smallest amount, however,
and you are as far from it as heaven is from earth.

I say, "A Jain friend told me recently that the Jains have a practice for teaching you to let go before you die. Some months before you die, you list all the foods that you usually eat, and you give them up one at a time. So you might start with chocolate, not eating chocolate ever again. And then, some time later, you add cauliflower. Then coffee. One by one, you give it all up, until you are just drinking water. By that time, letting go is probably pretty easy."

We're quiet for a while. I remember one of the many retreats we taught together at Omega Institute, where we had a bonfire with people chanting and throwing pinecones into the fire. The pinecones represented what they were attached to and wanted to give up.

Ram Dass says, "Even after you have given up attachment to specific people and things, there is also the attachment to life itself, the desire to keep on living."

Our talks have freed me in a major way from attachment to my own life and to Ram Dass's. But just a few months ago, we taught a retreat together called "Open Your Heart in Paradise," along with dharma teachers Jack Kornfield and Trudy Goodman. On the last day, I taught compassion practices in the morning. I had people partner up and then led them in contemplating phrases like "This person has suffered, just like me," "This person wants to be loved, just like me," and "This person will die, just like me." It was quite intense for many who did it, and I could feel a range of emotions in the room.

Next was what we call the Mala Ceremony, which we do at the end of each retreat. Ram Dass sits next to a picture of Maharaj-ji, while Krishna Das leads chanting. Each one of the

375 people at this retreat took a turn coming forward, and Ram Dass gave each a *mala* (the bracelet of beads to be fingered while repeating a mantra or the name of God) tied with a thread from one of Maharaj-ji's blankets. Maharaj-ji owned nothing but his blankets, and one of his few directives to us was "Say, 'Ram,'" the name of God.

It was a hot day, and the ceremony was long. After giving malas to about a hundred people, smiling and blessing each one, Ram Dass leaned his head to one side at an odd angle. He was surrounded by people: Ramesh handing out the malas, Perry taking photos, Ira walking each person up to Ram Dass. But Ram Dass's neck seemed to lose its strength, and his head fell all the way forward. In an instant, my experience went from one of loving support to silent panic: *Oh my God! Maybe this is it.* Someone handed Dassi a wet cloth, and she put it on Ram Dass's forehead. After a few interminable moments, he blinked and looked at her. She helped him back to center and gave him a cup of water. He smiled a small smile. After a little while, he wanted to resume the ritual. And it went on for another hour, one person after another. Dassi stayed very close with cold cloths and water. Ram Dass made it to the end, smiling. For some time, he looked at Maharaj-ji's picture, and then he went to his room to rest.

It could happen just like that, I think, recalling that incident. *It would probably be a great exit for Ram Dass, surrounded by so much love, feeling like he was doing Maharaj-ji's work, with a great Krishna Das soundtrack. But still . . .*

"Maharaj-ji said, 'Give up all desires.' That must include extending your life," I say. "But even if you give up the desire to have a long life, you should still take good care of yourself. Just don't be attached to the results."

LAST WORDS

I ask Ram Dass if he is thinking about last words. There is a tradition of spiritual teachers planning their last words. Zen masters compose a poem. Dilgo Khyentse Rinpoche said, "Never forget how swiftly this life will be over—like a flash of summer lightning or the wave of a hand." Ramakrishna said, "O mind, do not worry about the body. Let the body and its pain take care of each other. Think of the Holy Mother and be happy." The Buddha said, "Everything is subject to change. Remember to practice the teachings earnestly." The Sixteenth Karmapa, Rangjung Rigpe Dorje, said about death, "Nothing happens."

Ram Dass responds, "I think, first, if you have something important to say, say it now. Say you love someone now. Forgive someone now. Don't wait. Second, live in the moment. Know that moments are not in time. They are not in the world of the clock, the changing seasons, the process of growing old. Moments are in soul time. Live in the soul. Then you'll be ready for the moment of death. As you get closer to death, your intuition gets stronger. You'll know when you are getting closer. Forgive yourself and others. When Christ says, 'I am making all things new,' it's the same as living in the here and now and starting fresh in every moment. When you are really in this moment, everything is new, and the moment of death is just another moment."

WITHOUT WARNING

I take a break and walk through the garden, noticing the ripe papayas. When I go back upstairs, Ram Dass is waiting for me and right away says, "I was reading a book by a person who had a near-death experience after a motorcycle accident, and I keep thinking of friends who died on motorcycles. Owsley [Stanley], Shyamdas, Bo Lozoff. . . . Death can come without warning. You have to be ready. Gandhi, who had done much spiritual practice in his life, walked into a garden to give a press conference and was assassinated. As he fell, all he said was 'Ram.' He was ready."

I ask, "Have you ever thought you were about to die?"

"Yup," Ram Dass answers, "in my plane."

"Were you saying 'Ram'?"

"No. I was looking at the instruments and blaming myself for getting us into the situation."

THE LAST MOMENT

I n many spiritual traditions," Ram Dass tells me, "the state of consciousness at the last moment of life is considered so crucial that you spend your whole life preparing for it. There is a story of an old Zen monk who was dying. He had finished everything and was sure he was free, that he would get off the wheel of existence. He was floating away, free in his pure Buddha mind, when a thought arose of a beautiful deer he once saw in a field. He held on to that thought for a second because of its beauty. Well, he took birth again as a deer. It's as subtle as that."

I say, "There is a similar story about Maharaj-ji. Maharaj-ji is in a little temple by the side of the road. He eats his meal at ten thirty at night, before he goes to sleep. He's there with a *pujari* [a priest] and some women he called 'the Mas,' hanging around attending to things. Around one o'clock, Maharaj-ji calls out, 'I want dal and chapatis' [lentils and flat bread]."

"I know this story," Ram Dass says.

"Then tell me the rest."

"One of the Mas comes in and says, 'Maharaj-ji, you just ate a few hours ago.' But he says, 'I want dal and chapatis!' In the West, we'd probably think, *Oh, poor Maharaj-ji! He's really lost it; after all, he is in his seventies.* But in India, they think, *Who can understand the guru?* So they build the fire and make the dal and chapatis, and at two o'clock he eats voraciously, like he's never seen food before. He goes to sleep, and the next day a telegram arrives from the Plains, some hundreds of miles away. It says that the night before, at two in the morning, one of his devotees died. Maharaj-ji says to them, 'See? That's why I wanted the dal and chapatis.' But they don't understand, so they start to hound him: 'Maharaj-ji, tell us, why did you eat the dal and chapatis?' Maharaj-ji looks at them as if he is talking to schoolchildren: 'Don't you see? As he was dying, he wanted dal and chapatis, and I didn't want him to have to take another birth just for that.'"

Ram Dass continues, "However you think about it, you have to let go of your name, your history, your friends, your body, your intellect, your desire for beauty—and become one with your individual soul, because death is the extinction of your self. It's the death of who you know yourself to be, and there is no way the mind can grapple with the extinction of itself.

"Mindfulness and meditation are good ways to stabilize the mind, to learn to meet each thought and sensation as it arises, not clinging through either attraction or aversion, but bringing yourself back, over and over, to clear awareness. From your mind, you come into your heart, and from the heart, you will be able to become one with soul. You are not this disintegrating body. You are not becoming nothing. You are soul, and soul has life without limit."

I recall, "Years ago, when I was still young and not thinking much about death, Kalu Rinpoche came to stay at our house. I asked him why we should meditate, and he said, 'To prepare for death.' It seemed like a strange answer then, but now it makes perfect sense."

"I have come to understand death as a rite of passage," Ram Dass says. "We start out identified with the body and ego. Then, as we let go of the physical plane and begin to identify with soul, we can be helped by having people with us who are loving, who have faith in the process, and who know it is absolutely safe. They are there wishing us well, being love, talking among themselves about all the wonderful things we have done in this life, to help our mind be positive.

"The soul has experienced many deaths, so the more gracefully and fully you can identify with soul, the less you will fear. At the moment of death, you engage the deepest mysteries of the universe—you may do your most profound spiritual work in your last few minutes. Whether or not you believe in reincarnation or even heaven, prepare yourself by letting go of self-judgment and regret to be as peaceful, receptive, and loving as possible during your last moment."

GETTING READY

Ram Dass says, "Tibetan Buddhists talk a lot about the transition. They teach that as we approach death, the five elements that formed and sustained our body begin to dissolve: earth, air, fire, water, space. When the body begins to lose strength and feels drained of energy, when we feel like we are falling, sinking, and become weak and frail, the earth element is withdrawing. When we begin to lose control of bodily fluids, the water element is dissolving. When our mouth and nose dry up, when all the warmth of our body begins to leave and the breath is cold, when sound and sight are confused, this is the fire element dissolving into air. Then, when it becomes harder and harder to breathe, the air element is leaving. When the element of space withdraws, mind consciousness dissolves and breathing stops. We are returning to our original state, our true nature, Soul."

"Gelek Rimpoche said that you want to prepare to be like a bird sitting on a rock, ready to fly, with nothing holding you back. What do you think is the best way to prepare?" I ask.

Right away Ram Dass says, "Meditate to learn to be in the moment." And then, after some time, he adds, "Being in nature is helpful. Sitting in a forest, looking at the fallen trees and other things that are rotting, at new shoots growing, at everything changing, at flowers blooming and dying. We are part of nature. Trees and flowers don't resist death.

"Another helpful practice is scanning your body, as you would in a deep relaxation meditation, but instead of relaxing, you are letting go of attachment. Starting at the top of the body, bringing awareness to your eyes, you silently say, 'I am not these eyes and what they see. I am loving awareness.' You pause, breathing in and out of your heart, resting in loving awareness. And then, 'I am not these ears and what they hear. I am loving awareness. I am not this mouth and what it tastes. I am loving awareness.' And so on. You continue through the body, ending with 'I am not this body. I am loving awareness.' You can extend this practice to thoughts, memories, emotions, ideas: 'I am not these thoughts' and so on."

Then Ram Dass adds, "I expect my own death to be a wild ride with Maharaj-ji at the end. I'll go through some experiences, but he'll be there waiting. I expect to do a meditation on the guru as I am dying, to prepare myself for that reunion. You can do it by choosing the spiritual teacher closest to you, the being to whom you feel most attuned, such as Christ, Mary, Muhammad, Ram, Hanuman, an angel, Anandamayi Ma, Maharaj-ji, or your personal teacher or guru. Focus on them just as you would on your breath. This being is radiant, luminous, filled with compassion. You feel this being radiating with the wisdom that comes from an intimate harmony with the universe. Imagine that being coming into your body through the crown of your head. Imagine that your soul is inseparable from your teacher's. Experience the love radiating from your union. You are loving awareness."

AFTER DEATH

Never the spirit was born;
the spirit shall cease to be never.
Never was time it was not;
End and Beginning are dreams.

BHAGAVAD GITA

LET GO BEFORE YOU DIE

The next morning Ram Dass comes down to breakfast on his chair elevator. He looks sad and says, "Kush died last night. He was such a good cat." I know it is hard. Kush had been with Ram Dass for thirteen years. For the last several years, he had slept on Ram Dass's chest every night, breathing together with him. "He was one of my spiritual guides," Ram Dass says. "We vowed to let him die in his own way, not get shots to hasten it. And he did." We all feel sad. Later that day, we will bury Kush in the garden, chanting his way to his afterlife.

After breakfast, I walk down the road from Ram Dass's house. My heart is with Kush, but my body feels good striding along; I've been sitting a lot. It's cool for Maui, a good temperature for walking. I wave to two workmen landscaping a neighbor's property, hauling dead palm fronds into the back of a truck, trimming the grass around the base of the trees. The activity of life. *Aloha kakahiaka!* Their dog runs out to sniff me and wiggle his ears. I pet him and smile. The ordinary moments of life are becoming more precious.

When I get back, I decide to listen to a talk Ram Dass once gave about what happens after death.

When you die, where your consciousness is at the moment of death is a reflection of your level of evolution. If you are ready for the transformation that occurs at the moment of death, when there is a dissolving of the control mechanism and an intensification of all the energies, and you are not identified with all that so that you have equanimity through it, you can witness from a place of presence. You can witness the entire process of dying, and your consciousness doesn't flicker. Most people, however, are attached to some way of looking at the world, and when that starts to dissolve at the moment of death, they go unconscious. They go through the process unconsciously and pick up the thread later on, because it happens too fast and requires letting go too fast. So the art is to let go before you die, so that when you die, there is no letting go required. That's the most evolved state.

They say in the literature that one who sees the way in the morning can gladly die in the evening. Die before you die, so that when you die you need not die. There is a great quote from Kabir: 'If you don't break your ropes while you are

alive'—that is, if you don't break the identification with your body and your personality while you're alive—'do you think that ghosts will do it after?'

The idea that the soul will join with the ecstatic just because the body is rotten, that is all fantasy. What is found now is found then. If you find nothing now, you'll simply end up with an apartment in the city of death. But if you make love with the Divine now, then in the next life, you will have the face of satisfied desire. So plunge into the truth. Find out who your teacher is. Believe in the great sound. In other words, do your sadhana so that you can break the identification now. Then, at the moment of transformation, you can just go. If you have fear, you will be met and guided and protected. There will be beings that are there, who are on other planes, available to give meaning to this transformation for you.

So the least conscious beings go unconscious and get reprogrammed. The next more conscious beings meet other beings who guide them and help them. The most conscious beings just let go completely at the moment of death, and they don't go through more incarnations. The meaning of the wheel of birth and death is that as you get more and more evolved, there is less likelihood that you will keep taking rebirth. From the soul's point of view, you take rebirth only to work your way out of the illusion of your own separateness.

GOING HOME

When I finish listening and taking notes, I get the *Maui News* and bring it to Ram Dass in his room. I think it might be too early in the morning to talk about death, but he is reading a book on near-death experiences. He says, "I think it's like finally coming home, home to an old friend who had always known me and who loved me completely. It will be where I am supposed to be, at last."

Ram Dass sounds like he is giving travel instructions for journeying to our true home. "I want to go there," I say, and I mean it.

"I've wanted to go for a while now," Ram Dass says. "Sometimes I have to work to stay here." He is quiet for a while and then continues, "I know our home in this world is not our real home, that it's a temporary shelter, and that as much as we like it, we will have to give it up. Our real home is in the soul. Awareness of death is a way to awaken to this truth and to lead a happier life."

Almost everyone in the West who has reported a near-death experience tells of a loving, light-filled return to the Source, the home of the soul. They report an experience of wholeness outside time and space, not a place to be feared.

I say, "I like this description from *A Course in Miracles*":

> Beyond the body, beyond the sun and stars, past everything you see and yet somehow familiar, is an arc of golden light that stretches as you look into a great and shining circle. And all the circle fills with light before your eyes. The edges of the circle disappear, and what is in it is no longer contained at all. The light expands and covers everything, extending to infinity, forever shining and with no break or limit anywhere. Within it, everything is joined in perfect continuity. Nor is it possible to imagine that anything could be outside, for there is nowhere that this light is not.[12]

THE SOUL POD

a while ago, after Larry and Girija Brilliant's son died, I had asked Ram Dass where he thought Jonathan was now. Ram Dass said that through death we all find our soul pod. Jon was with Maharaj-ji, in love, in his soul pod. I ask him now to say more about that.

Ram Dass speaks clearly, with certainty. I can tell he's been waiting to say this. "I've wondered for a long time about what happens after death. I have talked to teachers, I've read the spiritual texts, and I've read books by people who have had near-death experiences, like Ray Moody, who wrote *Life after Life*. I've also communicated with my friend Emmanuel, who is not in his body—he is a spirit that has spoken through Pat Rodegast. Emmanuel says death is completely safe; it's like taking off a tight shoe. It is some combination of all of these that seems to engender such conviction in me that all does not end at the moment of death—although it's obvious that I do not know what happens after death in the usual scientific sense.

"As a result of this, I have been able to work with the dying and bring to them, in the face of the unknown, qualities of equanimity and peace. In those moments of being with a person who is approaching death, I find that only truth works. And so I am forced to examine and reexamine the depths of my understanding of life after death. This is the crucible through which what I am going to share has passed.

"As you extricate yourself from a solid identification with body and with personality and with materiality, you begin to have the spaciousness to allow that death may be part of a process rather than the end. I feel that very deeply. People ask, 'Do you believe that there is continuity after death?' and I say, 'I don't believe it—it IS.' This offends my scientific friends to no end."

"What about consciousness at the moment of death?" I ask.

"Right now, I believe that at the moment of death, the thought forms to which we are attached determine what happens next. As Maharaj-ji said, 'If you desire a mango at the moment of death, you'll be born an insect. If you even desire the next breath, you will take birth again.' Because of this effect, cultures that believe in reincarnation pay much attention to preparing for the moment of death. The Tibetans, for example, describe how not to get stuck in the feeling of heaviness when the earth element leaves, or the experience of dryness when the water element leaves, or the experience of coldness when the heat element leaves, or the feeling that the out breath is longer than the in breath as the air element leaves.

"I don't have a [mental] picture of the bardos, the transitional states between death and rebirth that the Tibetans describe, but I imagine they are true. What I do feel with confidence is that when we die, we join our soul pod."

"Our soul pod?" I ask.

"This is how I understand it. When we die, we leave our ego and body behind, but the soul goes on. Once it is free of the ego and the body, the soul merges back into the oceanic whole, into the One. Think of the cyclic process of the ocean mist rising off of the ocean, forming clouds, turning to raindrops falling into the ocean. The ocean is made of raindrops, but it is also the one ocean. It is an infinite and eternal space of love.

"We have been born and died so many times. Remember that story the Buddha told about a mountain six miles wide and six miles high. A bird flies over the mountain once every hundred years with a silk scarf in its beak that brushes the tip of the mountain. The length of time it takes the scarf to wear away the mountain is how long we have been doing this. Once every hundred years, the scarf goes over. A scarf and a mountain. It goes on and on and on.

"And each time we die, we find our soul pod. It's home. It's outside time and space. Much of my life has been about trying to make contact with this home. I've come home at times, through drugs, through meditation, and most powerfully through being with Maharaj-ji, but it has always been temporary. I look forward to nestling in to home through this new beginning."

"Who is at home in the soul pod?" I ask.

"The soul pod is all friendly souls who love each other, souls we've been together with through many lifetimes. We recognize them because they feel familiar. Love for them is like air for us—they live on love. They welcome you tenderly and ask, 'What was your incarnation like? What did you learn?' The sharing is beautiful. I think that in this incarnation in the West, we have learned a lot about individuality—of people, families, tribes, and nations—and how it breeds separation, which leads to fear.

"The souls in the soul pod are beings of light. The brightest light in the pod is your guru, or guide, who knows everything about your past incarnations and gives you guidance for the next.

"I have faith that Maharaj-ji will be the brightest light in my soul pod. I imagine my soul standing beside him, laughing at the melodrama on earth as we witness it. He and I will pick the most suitable incarnation for me so that I can learn the most from my karma in the next life. And there will be other very loving beings who have been significant to me, because we are all in this together, parallel souls on a parallel journey of finding meaning and eventually releasing meaning in order to surrender into the One."

The room feels a little like a soul pod right now. Wind blows through the palms outside. Birds are chirping *tee-cho, tee-cho, tee-cho*.

GETTING CLOSER

Frank Ostaseski is visiting today, and we all have lunch together. We are trying out a new diet with breadfruit, rutabagas, and salad. Frank tells Ram Dass that he is deeply moved by his advice to love your past no matter what it is; no matter how painful, to see your life as a story and simply love it without judgment.

Ram Dass responds, "You may see that you could have done some things better, but the core practice is to love it all, to accept it all, to love yourself and your story."

There are tears in Frank's blue eyes.

"Everything is lovable," says Ram Dass.

Later, after lunch, I go upstairs for one last conversation. We've reached the soul pod, so there's not much left to say. *We should act like we're in a soul pod already*, I am thinking, *being loving and helpful to each other, learning together, seeing each other as longtime companions walking each other home.*

Ram Dass says, "You know, all this talk about my own death, about the hearse and the funeral pyre—it's deepened my personal relationship to death. In prep school, I played the funeral director in Thornton Wilder's play *Our Town*. Now, every time I go by a cemetery, I have feelings about my own death."

I realize I am closer to it too.

Then Ram Dass says, "I'm changing. We are changing. Do you think so?"

"Yes, we are," I answer. "Every time I visit, you are more transparent, more loving, more wise . . ."

"My mind isn't getting in the way of my heart," he says. "It's love. Love conquered my mind."

It's time for dinner. As I open the door to leave, Ram Dass calls out, "I love you."

"I love you too," I answer.

EPILOGUE

A few weeks after we finished the last conversation, there was an early morning emergency alert in Hawaii, mistakenly warning of an incoming ballistic missile attack. The alarm set off widespread panic in a state that was already on edge because of escalating tensions between the United States and North Korea. Although the alert was a mistake, it took seventeen minutes for the governor to let people know because he couldn't remember his Twitter password. In those minutes, everyone in Hawaii faced the possibility of imminent death.

When I talked to Ram Dass, he said, "It was an interesting situation; everyone was focused on what matters. Some freaked out, left their cars in the road, and ran. Some were out at sea and were frantically paddling back to shore."

Lakshman, who was off island at the time, said, "I would have tried to meditate but would probably have called my family and then burst into tears and wailed, 'I don't wanna die!'"

"What did you do?" I asked Ram Dass.

"We were getting ready for chanting in the living room. I felt very calm. I wasn't thinking about the future. I was in the present moment. I was in my soul, with Maharaj-ji."

Dassi said, "Ram Dass was very peaceful, and as a result everyone here was calm. It was a feeling of letting go. It was beautiful."

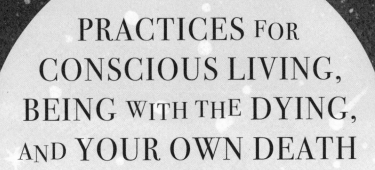

PRACTICES FOR CONSCIOUS LIVING, BEING WITH THE DYING, AND YOUR OWN DEATH

You are not dead yet. It's not too late
to open your depths by plunging into them
and drink in the life
that reveals itself quietly there.

RAINER MARIA RILKE

PRACTICES FOR CONSCIOUS LIVING
AND A LOVING HEART

READING THE WISDOM HOLDERS

Ram Dass suggests that if you think you don't understand enough, you may want to read and study. "In *Be Here Now*, I called it 'Books to Hang Out With.' These are books that are like friends. I don't know who your friends are, but my friends are Christ, the Buddha, Maharaj-ji, Ramana Maharshi, Ramakrishna, Lao Tzu, the Third Chinese Patriarch, Hazrat Inayat Khan, Solomon, and on and on. These are my buddies, a very elite group of people. If they shook your hand, would you know them any better than when you read a word that came from their heart? I can sit down, and if I am quiet and open, I can read the words of any of these beings and in a moment be at a whole new level of wisdom. So read the classics, the primary texts, and the great teachers."

For recommended contemporary books on dying and loving, see the resources section at the end of this book.

MEDITATION

If you do not have a regular meditation practice, set yourself a period of time to seriously try meditation, perhaps two weeks or a month in which you promise yourself that no matter what you experience in meditation, you will continue to do it regularly. The purpose of meditating is to cut through all your models of how you see the universe. In this way, you keep seeing everybody around you as if for the first time, again and again. When you're walking, you walk. When you're enjoying life, you enjoy. Become fully conscious in each moment. See the enjoyment, see that which is enjoyed, see that you are enjoying it. And be open to whatever experiences come in your meditation. Don't get fixated on a model of what meditation is supposed to feel like. Set aside judging, being critical, and having opinions. Meditation is about giving up models and labels.

The less you expect, the less you judge, and the less you cling to any experience as significant, the further you will progress. What you are seeking is a transformation of your being far beyond that which any specific experience can give you. It is important to expect nothing and be ready for anything, to take every experience—including the negative ones—as merely a step on the path, and to proceed.

Some people find meditation boring. They feel as if nothing is happening. This is another way in which the old you holds on tight, and it is important to be able to persist even through the experiences of boredom.

On the other hand, your initial reaction to meditation may be just the opposite of boredom—you may find ecstasy. Many people find things happening during meditation that give them incredible enthusiasm and truly ecstatic states. I suggest that in the early stages you move gently and slowly. Don't overreact. Positive experiences may well be followed by indifference. It is wise in all stages of meditation to be calm and not to make too much of any of your experiences, positive or negative. Merely notice them and keep on with your meditation practice.

When you are in the moment, time slows down. In this moment, you have all the time in the world. But don't waste a moment. Who you really are is beyond time. Live in the here and now, and start fresh in every new moment.

MEDITATION INSTRUCTION

Sit quietly. Just be with what is. If you're hot, be hot. If some part of you hurts, let it hurt. If you're emotionally open, let yourself be emotionally open, and if you're closed, be closed. If you're bored, be bored, and if you're stimulated, be stimulated. Just let it all be.

Bring your awareness to your breath. Breathe in and out naturally, just noticing the breath itself as it comes in and out of your nostrils, not trying to change it. Notice its texture, temperature, duration. When your attention wanders, as it will, simply return to the breath. Do this until your mind and body begin to settle into a calm, quiet, stable state.

Now, imagine a vast sky before you, and crossing it are clouds, coming into your vision and going out of your vision. The sky is vast and present, the clouds, coming and going. Imagine now that the sky is mirrored within you, so that inside of you is a vast sky, right in the middle of your chest. And every thought you have, every sensation you have, every model you have of who you are or what it's all about, see all of that now as clouds, coming and going, rising in your mind and then disappearing, rising in your body and then disappearing. And keep focusing on the sky, on the vast sky that is not changed in any way by the clouds.

Now, imagine an immense ocean. Rising up out of the ocean are waves. The waves rise, and then they dissolve back into the ocean. Be the vast ocean of awareness, letting thoughts, sensations, plans, memories, hopes, fears, life, and death all be waves that rise up out of your awareness and sink back into your awareness. Cultivate resting in awareness. No coming, no going. No birth, no death. Just vast ocean.

When you have learned to rest in that part of your being, pure awareness, pure is-ness, pure consciousness, pure love, beyond form, just vast presence, then notice what arises: *ah!* life . . . *ah!* death . . . *ah!* coming . . . *ah!* going . . . *ah!* joy . . . *ah!* sadness. All of it.

When you know that quality of your being—the ocean, the sky, the awareness—you are free. And being free, you can dance the dance of life and the dance of death. May all beings in this very life be free.

MINDFULNESS INSTRUCTION

In Chinese, the word for "mindfulness" is a composite: the character for "now" is drawn atop the character for "heart/mind."

Mindfulness is both a process (mindfulness practice) and an outcome (mindful awareness). It begins with the simple act of paying attention with care and respect. Mindful practices are found in many traditions all around the globe. The word *mindfulness* can mean something very particular in each of these traditions, so as a shorthand definition, many use the one inspired by Jon Kabat-Zinn, founder of the Center for Mindfulness in Medicine, Health Care, and Society and creator of the Mindfulness-Based Stress Reduction program: it is the awareness that arises by nonjudgmentally paying attention on purpose in the present moment.

It is a way of being in which one is highly aware (of what is inside yourself and outside yourself in the environment) and focused on the reality of the present moment, accepting and acknowledging it, without getting caught up in thoughts about the situation or emotional reactions to the situation. It is a capability we can all cultivate. Mindful awareness allows us to observe our mental states without overidentifying with them, creating an attitude of acceptance that can lead to greater curiosity and better self-understanding.

Begin by sitting in a chair or on a cushion on the floor, with your back straight but relaxed. Either close your eyes or rest them with a soft gaze on a point nearby. Relax into your sitting posture with a few deep breaths. Allow the body and mind to become utterly relaxed while remaining alert. Sweep your awareness through your body, feeling the sensations that are present with no agenda, no goal, just staying mindful of these sensations.

After some time, shift your awareness to the field of sound vibrations. Be aware of both the pure sound vibrations as well as the space or silence between the sounds. As with body sensations, incline your awareness away from the definition of a sound or thoughts about a sound and simply attune to a sound just as it is.

After some minutes of awareness of body and sounds, bring your attention to your natural breathing process. Locate the area in the body where the breath is most clear and let awareness lightly rest there. For some, it is the sensation of the rising and falling of the abdomen; for others, it may be the sensations experienced at the nostrils with each inhalation and exhalation. Let the breath breathe itself without control, direction, or force. Feel the full breath cycle, from the beginning through the middle to the end.

Your awareness is a combination of receptivity, like listening, and alertness, attentive presence. Let go of everything else, or let it be in the background. Just let the breathing breathe itself. As soon as you notice the mind wandering off, losing itself in thought, be aware of that without judging and gently return your attention to your breath.

AN ABBREVIATED MINDFULNESS INSTRUCTION

Breathe normally. Pay attention to the breath as it enters through your nostrils, fills your lungs, and then flows back out of your body. When thoughts, emotions, or sensations arise and you lose awareness of your breath, bring your awareness gently back to the breath and begin again.

RAM DASS'S GURU MEDITATION

I look at Maharaj-ji's picture, and I go with the Big Maharaj-ji, not Maharaj-ji as I knew him in India. I meet him in my imagination and converse with him, but not in words. In karma yoga, you deal with the experience in front of you. Maharaj-ji doesn't react to my "achievements." He is simply there with constant love. He brings me to another plane of consciousness, a oneness, the atman. Sometimes I cry.

LOVING AWARENESS

How does one become loving awareness? Ram Dass says, "I change my identification from the ego to the soul. I shift from my head, the thought of who I am, to my spiritual heart, feeling directly, intuiting, becoming loving awareness. It's a change from a worldly outer identification to a spiritual inner identification. You can practice it in any moment, including when you are dying."

LOVING AWARENESS INSTRUCTION

Concentrate on your spiritual heart, right in the middle of your chest. Breathe in and out of your heart, repeating the phrase, "I am loving awareness. I am loving awareness. I am loving awareness . . . loving awareness . . . loving awareness." Remember that it's always right here. Enter into the flow of love with a quiet mind and see all things as part of yourself.

INSTRUCTION FOR REMEMBERING DEATH

Every morning and every evening, I calm my heart by contemplating death,
considering myself as dead. Then I am able to live as though my
body were already dead, and I am freed to live well.

BUSHIDO: THE WAY OF THE WARRIOR

Each day for a few minutes, simply remember death. You can say to yourself, "All beings die. I will die too." Or you could simply think about how you would like to die, what is important for you to do and be before you die. You might also remember loved ones who have died. Just find a way to bring death into your awareness every day. Remember death for a few minutes before or after your daily practice. You could program a reminder into your phone or your computer; maybe put a note next to your bed. The app WeCroak will send you five notifications a day, quotes on dying from a wide range of sources. You can also write short entries in a journal.

GRATITUDE PRACTICE

The great open secret of gratitude is that it does not depend on external circumstance. It's like a setting or a channel that we can switch to at any moment, no matter what's going on around us. It helps us connect to our basic right to be here, the way the breath does. It's a stance of the soul. Gratitude is the kernel that can flower into everything we need to know.

Sit quietly and close your eyes. Bring to mind the past day. Walk through it, hour by hour or minute by minute, noticing what you are grateful for: friends, family, clouds, trees, a loving email, a memory of childhood, watermelon, being alive. Breathe in and out with full, deep breaths.

RAM DASS'S FOOD BLESSING

It's interesting that something that was for many of us a time of impatience during childhood, when adults were controlling the situation, can later become a moment to reawaken to living truth again, a moment of appreciating life. There are many ways to bless food. If you have a familiar way, work with that. I hold the food out in front of me, or I just sit with my hands around the food. The blessing I use is a Sanskrit prayer:

Brahmarpanam Brahma Havir
Brahmagnau Brahmanaahutam
Brahmaiva Tena Ghantavyam
Brahmakarma Samadhina

   I say the words in Sanskrit and then think about them for a moment. Food is part of the One. It's part of God, part of all form, part of the natural law, part of the universe. Making this prayer and offering the food, I am part of God, the food is part of God, and my hunger and the fire with which the food is cooked are also part of God. I use just this prayer to remind myself, to bring myself home, and I begin to sense the oneness of everything.

KIRTAN

Kirtan, or chanting, is a part of the path of devotional yoga, also known as bhakti yoga. Krishna Das, one of the foremost kirtan leaders in the West, has this to say about the practice: "The words of these chants are called the divine names, and they come from a place that's deeper than our hearts and our thoughts, deeper than the mind. And so, as we sing them, they turn us toward ourselves and into ourselves. They bring us in, and as we offer ourselves into the experience, the experience changes us. These chants have no meaning other than the experience we have when chanting them. Although chanting comes from the Hindu tradition, it's not about being a Hindu or believing anything in advance. It's just about doing it and experiencing. You just sit down and sing."

You will find some recommended kirtan CDs in the resources section at the end of this book.

LOVINGKINDNESS MEDITATION INSTRUCTION

Find a comfortable posture. One of the aims in this meditation is to feel good, so make your posture relaxed and comfortable. Then begin to focus your attention around the solar plexus and your chest area—your "heart center." Breathe lovingkindness in and out of that area, as if all experience is happening from there. Anchor your mindfulness only on the sensations at your heart center.

Begin by generating a feeling of kindness toward yourself, and as you continue to breathe in and out, use one of these traditional phrases or another you choose yourself. Say or think them several times.

May I be free from inner and outer harm and danger.
May I be safe and protected.
May I be free of mental suffering and distress. May I be happy.
May I be free of physical pain and suffering. May I be healthy and strong.
May I be able to live in this world happily, peacefully, joyfully, with ease.

Next, direct your attention to a person who most invites a feeling of pure, unconditional lovingkindness in you. The first person is usually a mentor, a benefactor, an elder, a parent. Repeat the phrases for this person now: *May you be safe and protected* . . .

After feeling strong unconditional love for this first person, focus your attention on a person you regard as a dear friend and repeat the phrases again for this person, breathing in and out of your heart center.

Then move on to a neutral person, someone for whom you feel neither strong like nor dislike. As you repeat the phrases for this person, allow yourself to feel tenderness and loving care for their welfare.

Next, focus on someone with whom you have difficulty, and repeat the phrases for this person. If you have trouble doing this, before each phrase you can say, *To the best of my ability, I wish that you be* . . . If you begin to feel ill will toward this person, return to the first benefactor and let the lovingkindness arise again. Then return to this difficult person.

After meditating on the difficult person, radiate lovingkindness to all beings: *May all beings be safe, happy, healthy, live joyously, with ease.*

JUST-LIKE-ME COMPASSION MEDITATION

Realizing that the other person is also just like me
is the basis on which we can develop compassion,
not only toward those around us but also toward our enemy.
Normally, when we think about our enemy, we think about harming him.
Instead, try to remember that the enemy is also a human being, just like you.

HIS HOLINESS THE FOURTEENTH DALAI LAMA

This practice can be done alone, by bringing to mind a friend, a colleague, a neutral person, or a difficult person. It can also be done silently, when meeting someone new. This practice is also effective when done with a group of people. Ask participants to sit in pairs or have them stand in two lines facing one another. Have the people look into their partners' eyes, letting them know that they can close their eyes or look down at any time if they need to. If practicing in a group, after participants complete the exercise with one partner, have them begin again with a new partner, so that the repetition with someone new increases everyone's understanding that all others are "just like me."

Use any or all of the suggested phrases below or any others that may be more appropriate.

Begin by becoming aware that there is a person in front of you, another human being, just like you. Then, silently repeat the phrases below, while looking at your partner:

This person has a body and a mind, just like me.
This person has feelings, emotions, and thoughts, just like me.
This person has experienced physical and emotional pain and suffering, just like me.
This person has at some time been sad, disappointed, angry, or hurt, just like me.

This person has felt unworthy or inadequate, just like me.

This person worries and is frightened sometimes, just like me.

This person will die, just like me.

This person has longed for friendship, just like me.

This person is learning about life, just like me.

This person wants to be caring and kind to others, just like me.

This person wants to be content with what life has given them, just like me.

This person wishes to be free from pain and suffering, just like me.

This person wishes to be safe and healthy, just like me.

This person wishes to be happy, just like me.

This person wishes to be loved, just like me.

Now, allow wishes for well-being to arise:

I wish this person to have the strength, resources, and social support they need to navigate the difficulties in life with ease.

I wish this person to be free from pain and suffering.

I wish this person to be peaceful and happy.

I wish this person to be loved . . . because this person is a fellow human being, just like me.

After a few moments, thank your partner with a bow or in whatever way feels appropriate.

SPIRITUAL LEGACY

The idea of an ethical or a spiritual legacy, as opposed to the material goods we leave behind, can be traced back to the first book of the Jewish and Christian Bibles, in which the dying Jacob gives his children what in Hebrew is called his *tzava'ah*, or spiritual estate. Passing along the wisdom, advice, and blessings of elders is a familiar tradition in other cultures as well. Native American friends tell of grandparents teaching children about the traditional ways so that they won't be lost.

But what exactly is worth passing on? And how do you do it? One way is to tell the story of your life, the story of what is most important to you and how you know it is important. Stories teach, stories heal, and they are easy to remember. The great contemplatives have all used parables to teach complex and paradoxical truths. And each one is connected to the bigger story.

SPIRITUAL LEGACY INSTRUCTION

Take some time for your favorite spiritual practice—whether it's meditation, yoga, mindful walking, chanting, or singing—to open yourself to the story that wants to tell itself. Then write it down or record it. Another approach is to ask a friend or a relative to ask you questions about your life. Don't worry about it being perfect. For example, one friend began her story this way: "I am from porches and grass and roast chicken and gravy smells and crickets and a green Girl Scout uniform." Another person wrote about the story of a struggle, saying, "Dear to my heart is this battle for the environment, but I am asking myself not what I am against but what I am for." Write whatever is important to you.

PRACTICES FOR BEING WITH THE DYING

DEALING WITH FEAR

Death is the ultimate fear. When sitting with the dying, it is important to be fearless so that you can help the dying person let go of their fear and die knowing that the process is perfectly safe. When you are afraid of something, come up as close to it as you comfortably can, and sit with it, watching your reactivity and resistance, seeing the boundaries, noticing the quality of the fear, seeing it as a process that comes from conditioning, from identification. When you get uncomfortable, stop and begin again, being gentle, not judging yourself.

You can also try this simple visualization to let go of fear and anxiety: Sit in a comfortable position, relaxed but alert. Close your eyes and breathe naturally. Bring to mind what it is you are currently afraid of. Look at the fears: fear of dying, fear of loss, fear of failure, anxiety about the future, and so on. Imagine each fear in the form of dense, thick smoke inside you, and breathe it out. Breathe out each fear, one by one. When breathing in, imagine pure and inspiring energy, love, and the fearlessness of wise beings filling your body and mind. Continue with this practice for anywhere between five and twenty minutes.

SHORT PRACTICE FOR DEALING WITH FEAR

Bring to mind what you are afraid of. Notice the sensations in your body and then make tight fists with your hands, feeling the fear in your hands, arms, and torso. Hold this for a few minutes. Then breathe a full, deep in breath, filling your body. On the out breath, slowly uncurl your fingers, with your palms facing up.

Relax, continue to breathe, and notice the sensations in your body. Smile.

BEING A LOVING ROCK

See pages 118–124 for a description of how to be a loving rock for the dying.

PRACTICES FOR YOUR OWN DEATH

Seeing into darkness is clarity. Knowing how to yield is strength.
Use your own light and return to the source of light.
This is called practicing eternity.

LAO TZU

INSTRUCTION FOR WELCOMING THE GUIDE

Sit or lie quietly, breathing naturally. When you feel ready, ask God, the Buddha, Mary, Kwan Yin, Tara, Jesus, Muhammad, or Truth to enter your body through the crown of your head and to become one with you. This being is radiant, luminous, and filled with compassion. Imagine that your souls are inseparable and experience the love radiating from your union. Ask this being to stay with you through your transition. Know that you are loving awareness.

PRAYER OR MANTRA

You can recite a prayer or a mantra as you begin the process of letting go and leaving the body. You can also ask others at your bedside to pray or to chant to help calm the soul. All religious and spiritual traditions have prayers or chants for this transition. For example, in Judaism the prayer is *Shema Yisrael, Adonai eloheinu, Adonai echad* (God is One. Go toward the One). In Hinduism we repeat *Om Namah Shivaya*, a chant that invokes Shiva, the god of transformation.

I AM NOT THIS BODY

This exercise is a form of body scan, but instead of simply noticing or relaxing, you are letting go of attachment. Start at the top of the body, bringing awareness to your eyes, and silently say, *I am not these eyes and what they see. I am loving awareness.*

Pause, breathing in and out of your heart center and resting in loving awareness. Then silently say, *I am not these ears and what they hear. I am loving awareness. I am not this mouth and what it tastes. I am loving awareness.* Continue in this way throughout the whole body, ending with *I am not this body. I am loving awareness.*

You can also extend this practice to thoughts, memories, emotions, and ideas: *I am not these thoughts . . . I am loving awareness.*

RECOMMENDED RESOURCES

BOOKS

Baldwin, James. *The Fire Next Time.* New York: Vintage Books, 1992.

Blackman, Sushila, ed. *Graceful Exits: How Great Beings Die.* Boston: Shambhala Publications, 2005.

Chödrön, Pema. *When Things Fall Apart: Heart Advice for Difficult Times.* Boulder, CO: Shambhala Publications, 2016.

Das, Krishna. *Chants of a Lifetime: Searching for a Heart of Gold.* Carlsbad, CA: Hay House, 2010.

Ellison, Koshin Paley, and Matt Weingast, eds. *Awake at the Bedside: Contemplative Teachings on Palliative and End-of-Life Care.* Somerville, MA: Wisdom Publications, 2016.

Fischer, Norman. *Sailing Home: Using the Wisdom of Homer's Odyssey to Navigate Life's Perils and Pitfalls.* Berkeley, CA: North Atlantic Books, 2011.

Fremantle, Francesca. *Luminous Emptiness: Understanding the Tibetan Book of the Dead.* Boston: Shambhala Publications, 2001.

Gawande, Atul. *Being Mortal: Medicine and What Matters in the End.* New York: Picador/Macmillan, 2015.

Gehlek Rimpoche. *Good Life, Good Death: Tibetan Wisdom on Reincarnation.* New York: Riverhead/Penguin, 2001.

Halifax, Joan. *Being with Dying: Cultivating Compassion and Fearlessness in the Presence of Death.* Boston: Shambhala Publications, 2008.

Holecek, Andrew. *Preparing to Die: Practical Advice and Spiritual Wisdom from the Tibetan Buddhist Tradition.* Boulder, CO: Snow Lion/Shambhala Publications, 2013.

Huxley, Aldous. *Island.* New York: Harper Perennial Modern Classics, 2009.

Kalanithi, Paul. *When Breath Becomes Air.* New York: Random House, 2016.

King, Martin Luther, Jr. *A Testament of Hope: The Essential Writings and Speeches*, ed. James M. Washington. New York: HarperOne, 2003.

Kübler-Ross, Elisabeth. *On Death and Dying: What the Dying Have to Teach Doctors, Nurses, Clergy & Their Own Families.* New York: Scribner, 2014.

Lama Surya Das. *The Big Questions: How to Find Your Own Answers to Life's Essential Mysteries.* New York: Rodale, 2007.

Lattin, Don. *Changing Our Minds: Psychedelic Sacraments and the New Psychotherapy.* Santa Fe, NM: Synergetic Press, 2017.

Levine, Stephen. *A Year to Live: How to Live This Year as If It Were Your Last.* New York: Three Rivers Press, 1998.

Levine, Stephen, and Ondrea Levine. *Who Dies? An Investigation of Conscious Living and Conscious Dying.* New York: Anchor, 1989.

Levy, Naomi. *Einstein and the Rabbi: Searching for the Soul.* New York: Flatiron Books, 2017.

Lief, Judith. *Making Friends with Death: A Buddhist Guide to Encountering Mortality.* Boston: Shambhala Publications, 2001.

Markus, Parvati. *Love Everyone: The Transcendent Wisdom of Neem Karoli Baba Told Through the Stories of the Westerners Whose Lives He Transformed.* New York: HarperOne, 2015.

Mascaro, Juan, trans. *The Bhagavad Gita.* New York: Penguin, 2003.

Nhat Hanh, Thich. *No Death, No Fear: Comforting Wisdom for Life.* New York: Riverhead/Penguin, 2002.

O'Donohue, John. *To Bless the Space Between Us: A Book of Blessings.* New York: Doubleday, 2008.

O'Hara, Enkyo Pat. *Most Intimate: A Zen Approach to Life's Challenges.* Boston: Shambhala Publications, 2014.

Ostaseski, Frank. *The Five Invitations: Discovering What Death Can Teach Us about Living Fully.* New York: Flatiron Books, 2017.

Ozeki, Ruth. *A Tale for the Time Being: A Novel.* New York: Penguin, 2013.

Rohr, Richard. *Falling Upward: A Spirituality for the Two Halves of Life.* San Francisco: Jossey-Bass, 2011.

Rosenberg, Larry. *Living in the Light of Death: On the Art of Being Truly Alive.* Boston: Shambhala Publications, 2000.

Salzberg, Sharon. *Real Love: The Art of Mindful Connection.* New York: Flatiron Books, 2017.

Smith, Rodney. *Lessons from the Dying.* Boston: Wisdom Publications, 1998.

Thurman, Howard. *Meditations of the Heart.* Boston: Beacon Press, 1999.

Zajonc, Arthur. *Meditation as Contemplative Inquiry: When Knowing Becomes Love.* Great Barrington, MA: Lindisfarne Books, 2009.

CDS AND DOWNLOADS

Meditation

Chödrön, Pema, and Barbara Groth. *Good Medicine: How to Turn Pain into Compassion.* Boulder, CO: Sounds True, 2014.

Kabat-Zinn, Jon. *Mindfulness Meditation for Pain Relief: Guided Practices for Reclaiming Your Body and Your Life.* Boulder, CO: Sounds True, 2009.

Kirtan

Das, Krishna. *Heart as Wide as the World.* Nettwerk Records, 2010. This and other Krishna Das recordings and online courses can be found at krishnadas.com.

Govinda, Ananta, and Gopi Kallayil. *Kirtan Lounge: Nectar of Devotion.* Vedic Renaissance Productions, 2013. Find this recording and more at kallayil.com.

Rao, Nina. *Antarayaami—Knower of All Hearts.* Rare Earth Explorations, 2013. Available at krishnadas.com.

Uttal, Jai, and Ben Leinbach. *Loveland: Music for Dreaming and Awakening.* Sounds True, 2006. This and other Jai Uttal recordings can be found at jaiuttal.com.

Harp Music to Comfort the Dying

Schroeder-Sheker, Therese. *Rosa Mystica* and *In Dulci Jubilo.* Celestial Harmonies, 1992. These CDs demonstrate the power of music to soothe and transport.

LINKS

RamDass.org

The official home of Ram Dass's articles, media, podcasts, events, online courses, and more. You can also follow Ram Dass at facebook.com/babaramdass, at twitter.com/babaramdass, and on Instagram @babaramdass. You can access the Be Here Now podcast network at beherenownetwork.com.

mirabaibush.com

Mirabai Bush teaches contemplative practices and develops programs through the application of contemplative principles and values. She is also at facebook.com/mirabai.bush.

nkbashram.org

This is where you can find information about the Neem Karoli Baba Ashram located in Taos, New Mexico.

livingdying.org

The Living/Dying Project offers conscious and compassionate support in the spirit of mutual exploration to those facing life-threatening illness, to their caregivers, to those facing life's most difficult situations, and to anyone committed to spiritual transformation.

doorwayintolight.org

Doorway into Light provides conscious and compassionate responses to dying and death for people in Hawaii.

fiveinvitations.com

Frank Ostaseski maintains this resource on how maintaining an ever-present consciousness of death can bring us closer to our truest selves.

mettainstitute.org

This site contains information on integrating the spiritual dimensions of living, dying, and transformation through professional training and educational programs and materials.

upaya.org/being-with-dying

Roshi Joan Halifax and the Upaya Institute offer Zen Buddhist training for being with the dying.

chaliceofrepose.org

An outgrowth of Therese Schroeder-Sheker's work in music thanatology, the Chalice of Repose Project aims to lovingly care for the physical and spiritual needs of the dying with prescriptive music, making patient-care services available to individuals and loved ones during the weeks, days, and hours leading up to and including the moments of transition.

deathcafe.com

At Death Café, people drink tea, eat cake, and discuss death. The aim is to raise awareness about death in order to help people make the most of their lives.

FILMS AND VIDEOS

V. Owen Bush, producer, director, and Ram Dass, narrator. *Love Serve Remember: From "Be Here Now" to "Be Love Now."* Glowing Pictures, 2010, glowingpictures.com/#/w-ram-dass/. A short film that distills Ram Dass's teachings on love and also features two guided meditations.

Gay Dillingham, producer, director. *Dying to Know: Ram Dass & Timothy Leary.* CNS Communications, 2014, dyingtoknowmovie.com. This film centers on an intimate conversation between Ram Dass and Timothy Leary just a few months before Leary's death. It is an emotional, respectful good-bye between two lifelong companions, Harvard professors who became counterculture icons.

Mickey Lemle, director. *Ram Dass Fierce Grace.* Lemle Pictures, 2001, lemlepictures.com/film_RD.html. A feature-length documentary that shows the wisdom of Ram Dass as he uses his spiritual practices to deal with the effects of the massive stroke he suffered in 1997. *Newsweek* called it one of the five best nonfiction films of the year.

Derek Peck, director. *Ram Dass, Going Home.* Further Pictures, 2017, ramdassgoinghome.com/. Shortlisted for an Oscar nomination, this film is a profound and poetic encounter with Ram Dass at his home on Maui as he nears the end of his life.

ACKNOWLEDGMENTS

RAM DASS

Special thanks to those who taught me and inspired me about death and dying: Stephen Levine, Elisabeth Kübler-Ross, Dale Borglum, Frank Ostaseski, Roshi Joan Halifax, Frances Vaughan, Angeles Arrien, Zalman Schachter-Shalomi, and Bodhi and Leilah Be.

MIRABAI BUSH

Loving thanks to those who gave material support for me to fly back and forth so many times to Maui and spend the hours it took to craft our long and rambling conversations into this slim book: Bob Shapiro, Frank Peabody, Gina Sharpe, Bokara Legendre, Bo Shao, and Oleg Gorelik.

The first readers helped by offering both encouragement and critical comment: Helen Tworkov, who was writing about dying with Mingyur Rinpoche; Danny Goleman; Owen Bush. I first read some of it aloud at a retreat for the Sevettes, the founding women of Seva Foundation, whose wise opinions are always important to me, and you were incredibly helpful: Sunanda, Girija, Jahanara, Suzanne, Pat, Bev, and Pauline.

My fellow board members of Love Serve Remember, who help further Maharaj-ji's treasured teachings, thank you: Raghu, Ramesh, Gopal, Gagan.

Dassi Ma, Lakshman Moss, Lucian Davis, and Govinda Cobb, who were Ram Dass's caretakers during the time of these conversations, helped him be healthy and comfortable, well fed, and always loved.

Thanks to Tami Simon, longtime friend, through whose vision Sounds True has flourished. And to all those at Sounds True who worked to transform these Maui conversations into a book: Jade Lascelles, Kira Roark, Wendy Gardner, Jeff Mack, Jennifer Miles, Beth Skelley, Jennifer Brown, and Vesela Simic.

Bows to all my teachers, including Gelek Rimpoche, who died this year, and to my niece Lisa Khanna—we shared the many emotions and awakenings of the death of my sister Barbara.

And deepest thanks to my extended Western Mass family, who support and sustain me, especially my husband E. J. Lynch, my son V. Owen Bush, and my divine granddaughter, Dahlia Bush.

NOTES

1. Kenneth E. Vail III et al., "When Death Is Good for Life: Considering the Positive Trajectories of Terror Management," *Personality and Social Psychology Review* 16, no. 4 (April 2012): 303–29, doi: 10.1177/1088868312440046.

2. Mark Twain, *Following the Equator: A Journey around the World* (New York: Harper & Brothers, 1899), 174.

3. Anaïs Nin, *The Diary of Anaïs Nin, Vol. 1: 1931–1934* (Boston: Houghton Mifflin Harcourt, 1969), 190.

4. Norman Fischer, "Love = Wisdom = Buddha," *Shambhala Sun* (January 2015): 58.

5. Pema Chödrön, *When Things Fall Apart: Heart Advice for Difficult Times* (Boston: Shambhala Publications, 2000), 57.

6. Nina Wise, "Luck Disguised as Ordinary Life," *ninawise.com*, ninawise.com/luck-disguised-as-ordinary-life/.

7. Don Lattin, *Changing Our Minds: Psychedelic Sacraments and the New Psychotherapy* (Santa Fe, NM: Synergetic Press, 2017), 77.

8. Lattin, *Changing Our Minds*, 128.

9. Timothy Leary, *Flashbacks* (New York: Tarcher/Penguin, 1997), 141.

10. Aldous Huxley, *Island* (New York: Harper Perennial Modern Classics, 2009), 321.

11. Mike "Schwann" Kawitzky, "True Conversations with Terence McKenna, Kona, September 1999," *Global Webtrance* (personal website), webtrance.co.za/hawaii.htm.

12. Helen Schucman, "The Forgotten Song," *A Course in Miracles*, T-21.I.8 (Mill Valley, CA: Foundation for Inner Peace, 1992), 447.

ABOUT THE AUTHORS

RAM DASS, one of America's most beloved spiritual figures, has made his mark on the world by teaching the path of the heart and promoting service in the areas of social consciousness and care for the dying. Ram Dass first went to India in 1967. He was still Dr. Richard Alpert, an eminent Harvard psychologist and psychedelic pioneer with Dr. Timothy Leary. In India, he met his guru, Neem Karoli Baba, affectionately known as Maharaj-ji, who gave Ram Dass his name, which means "servant of God."

Upon his return from India, Ram Dass became a pivotal influence in our culture with the publication of *Be Here Now* in 1970. In fact, those words have become a catchphrase in people's lives for the past forty years. He followed with *Still Here* in 2004 and completed his trilogy with *Be Love Now* in 2011. He released a new book with coauthor Rameshwar Das entitled *Polishing the Mirror: How to Live from Your Spiritual Heart* in 2013.

Ram Dass's spirit has been a guiding light for four generations, carrying millions along the journey, helping to free them from their bonds as he works his way through his own. He now makes his home in Maui, teaches worldwide through his website RamDass.org, and continues the work of Neem Karoli Baba through his Love Serve Remember Foundation.

After living two years in India in the seventies with Ram Dass, Neem Karoli Baba, and Buddhist teachers, **MIRABAI BUSH** returned home to become a leader in exploring the use of contemplative practices in American institutions and professions with the goal of a more just, compassionate, and reflective society. She has taught with Ram Dass in many settings.

Mirabai cofounded Illuminations, Inc., based on principles of "right livelihood," foreshadowing the movement for socially responsible business. Her experience led, many years later, to co-creating Google's popular training Search Inside Yourself: Mindfulness-Based Emotional Intelligence.

Mirabai directed the Seva Foundation Guatemala Project in Mayan community development and sustainable agriculture for ten years, which, through quiet reflection and informed dialogue, engaged intuitive intelligence and professional experience in decision making.

As founding director of The Center for Contemplative Mind in Society, Mirabai led a diverse network of leaders from almost every sector of American life to systematically explore the potential contribution of contemplative practices on American civic life. The practices—meditation, yoga, contemplative prayer, deep listening, *Lectio Divina*, and others—were drawn from diverse wisdom traditions and adapted in programs specifically designed for the sectors of law, business, journalism, environment, social justice activism, biotech sciences, youth leadership, government, and philanthropy. In higher education, the center now supports a network of 8,000 faculty and administrators in developing contemplative pedagogy and epistemology—an integrated way of knowing that calls on the whole person rather than critical faculties alone.

Mirabai lives in Western Massachusetts with her husband E. J. Lynch. She is mother of filmmaker V. Owen Bush and grandmother of Dahlia Bush.

ABOUT SOUNDS TRUE

Sounds True is a multimedia publisher whose mission is to inspire and support personal transformation and spiritual awakening. Founded in 1985 and located in Boulder, Colorado, we work with many of the leading spiritual teachers, thinkers, healers, and visionary artists of our time. We strive with every title to preserve the essential "living wisdom" of the author or artist. It is our goal to create products that not only provide information to a reader or listener, but that also embody the quality of a wisdom transmission.

For those seeking genuine transformation, Sounds True is your trusted partner. At SoundsTrue.com you will find a wealth of free resources to support your journey, including exclusive weekly audio interviews, free downloads, interactive learning tools, and other special savings on all our titles.

To learn more, please visit SoundsTrue.com/freegifts or call us toll-free at 800.333.9185.

SOUNDS TRUE
many voices, one journey